When the Lord gives you
it empowers you to overcome every attack the
devil exposed is a devil defeated. In *Hell's Toxic Trio* Ryan
exposes a threefold demonic cord that many believers have not
yet discerned. He also shows you how it can be easily broken
with heaven's strategy. You can't see what you can't see, but this
book will open your eyes to the root of toxic attacks in your life.
Get this book!

—JENNIFER LeCLAIRE
SENIOR LEADER, AWAKENING HOUSE OF PRAYER

Ryan LeStrange has an unusual and unique mantle of apostolic/
prophetic revelation. He captures key issues hindering breakthrough, spiritual freedom, and inheritance. In *Hell's Toxic
Trio* he both explains the hindrances as well as shows how to
move into freedom. A much-needed book!

—BARBARA J. YODER
LEAD APOSTLE, SHEKINAH REGIONAL APOSTOLIC CENTER
BREAKTHROUGH APOSTOLIC MINISTRIES NETWORK

Ryan LeStrange's new book, *Hell's Toxic Trio*, has pressed all the
right buttons. As I read the manuscript, I kept saying, "Amen!
Oh, my! Yes! That's the truth!" He has taken the power of that
threefold cord and unraveled its grip, and like Samson of old,
we can finally break free of those fetters that bind.

—JOHN KILPATRICK
FOUNDING PASTOR, CHURCH OF HIS PRESENCE

Over the years, I have learned that there are certain pollutants
that are really dangerous to one's personal health and also to the
well-being of the body of Christ. Some stuff just seems to seep
into your being over a long and slow process, while other things
just get in your face and try to eat your lunch! As believers and

leaders in the body of Christ, we need to be on the alert because the enemy is like a roaring lion. Ryan LeStrange identifies three of these high-level pollutants in his book *Hell's Toxic Trio* and shows ways to cleanse the soul so you can emanate a clean and righteous spirit and even permeate the atmosphere around you. The only thing missing from this book is a warning label: "If you partake of these contents, you might react and spit out some old stuff!" This book can change you from the inside out!

—James W. Goll
Founder, God Encounters Ministries
Author, Equipper, Performing Artist,
Certified Life Language Trainer

Throughout church history God has been faithful to raise up apostolic and prophetic leaders in hours of confusion. For such a time as this Ryan LeStrange has been raised up. *Hell's Toxic Trio* is the *rhema* word for now! Not only does he expose the antichrist spirit, he points the reader to the feet of Jesus. This book will be considered a classic.

—Brian Williams
Founder and Senior Leader, Hope City

Are you fearful, anxious, or rejected? There is lasting healing for the wounded soul. In this powerful book apostle Ryan LeStrange delivers a revelatory remedy with typical refreshing candor. Through each page God will expose the toxic trio that has arrested the destinies of millions, and you will be catapulted into your divine fulfillment. As you read, release your faith and expect personal revival.

—Kynan Bridges
Pastor, Apostolic Leader, Best-Selling Author
Grace & Peace Global Fellowship

HELL'S
TOXIC TRIO

RYAN LeSTRANGE

CHARISMA
HOUSE

Most CHARISMA HOUSE BOOK GROUP products are available at special quantity discounts for bulk purchase for sales promotions, premiums, fund-raising, and educational needs. For details, write Charisma House Book Group, 600 Rinehart Road, Lake Mary, Florida 32746, or telephone (407) 333-0600.

HELL'S TOXIC TRIO by Ryan LeStrange
Published by Charisma House
Charisma Media/Charisma House Book Group
600 Rinehart Road
Lake Mary, Florida 32746
www.charismahouse.com

Cover design by Vincent Pirozzi
Design Director: Justin Evans

Visit the author's website at RyanLeStrange.com.

Library of Congress Cataloging-in-Publication Data:
An application to register this book for cataloging has been submitted to the Library of Congress.
International Standard Book Number: 978-1-62999-488-8
E-book ISBN: 978-1-62999-489-5

18 19 20 21 22 — 987654321
Printed in the United States of America

I dedicate this book to the radical warriors who have fought through so many attacks of the enemy! I dedicate it to the fearless— the pioneers and planters who forge ahead in spite of the opposition. In every kingdom assignment, whether it be family, business, or ministry, there will typically be spiritual resistance. Victory belongs to the brave! In order to do exploits, we must keep pressing. I commend all of those who have daringly faced the opposition and kept going. Your greatest days are ahead!

CONTENTS

Acknowledgments...xi

Foreword by John Eckhardt...........................xiii

Introduction..xvii

Chapter 1 The Reality of the Unseen Realm...............1

Chapter 2 The Power of the Anointing...................26

Chapter 3 Jezebel, the Spiritual Assassin.................52

Chapter 4 Jezebel's Seduction, Schemes, and Strategies.....69

Chapter 5 Casting Down the Demon Queen Jezebel.......86

Chapter 6 Python, the Heat-Seeking Deceiver...........109

Chapter 7 Breaking Python's Grip.....................125

Chapter 8 The DNA of the Religious Spirit.............143

Chapter 9 First-Love Lifestyle: Freedom From
          the Religious Spirit.........................164

Chapter 10 Enforcing the Kingdom: Living Free.........184

Notes..200

ACKNOWLEDGMENTS

THANKS TO MY forever love, the amazing Joy LeStrange, who fearlessly pioneers with me, and to my talented son, Joshua. Thanks to my mom, Eileen, and all of my extended family for all the love and support. Thank you to my staff and team, who work so hard to help me circle the globe with fire. Thanks to my editing team and those who help bring these writing projects together. Thank you to my supporters, friends, and partners for standing, believing, sowing, and building with me—it takes a team!

Thanks to all of those who have labored to build, enlarge, and expand the kingdom. Thanks to the generals who have gone ahead—we honor you. Thanks to those in my generation who have dared to carry the mandate of radical prophetic preaching, supernatural miracles, and nation-shaking faith—I am honored to serve alongside you. Thanks to the next generation for being brave and daring—I want to stand with, walk alongside, and partner with you to see a great awakening.

FOREWORD

RYAN LESTRANGE HAS a passion to see the church walk in power and liberty. He is committed to seeing the church experience revival and glory. There are evil spirits that attempt to block the church from experiencing God's best. In this book Ryan LeStrange exposes some of the strategies of darkness that prevent the church from experiencing the liberty of the Holy Spirit. Many leaders are not aware of the tremendous battle in the spirit realm between good and evil. We should not be ignorant of Satan's devices.

Ryan LeStrange is a fresh voice for revival, prayer, the apostolic ministry, and the prophetic ministry. He is ministering around the world, and he challenges believers to move in power and authority. He has a burden to see the church break free from controlling powers that stop and block revival. This book is a product of his determination to see the fire of revival burn continuously.

Every generation has authors who will help us break through for kingdom advancement. Ryan LeStrange has experienced the truths written in this book. He is not echoing what others have said but is giving fresh revelation for this new generation. There are thousands of believers worldwide who desire to see the church grow and experience God's choice blessings. If you desire these blessings, then take to heart the insight given in this book. I have dealt with the spirits of Jezebel and python. These are deadly enemies to leaders and churches worldwide.

There are many leaders who are not equipped to deal with these adversaries. I recommend this book to leaders and intercessors. A greater knowledge in this area is essential if we desire victory. Some of the truths in this book may be new to many, but consider what is said, and the Lord will give you understanding. Prayer is one of the most effective ways to overcome these opponents. There are powerful prayers in this book that will help any believer or church wage the good warfare.

Religious spirits can be very deceptive. These spirits are often difficult to discern because they are religious. We need discernment to separate the true from the false. Ryan exposes spirits that mask themselves as being from God but are from the enemy.

I have been a proponent of the prophetic ministry for many years. I have seen the great blessings prophets and prophetic people bring to the church. Ministries that embrace the prophetic ministry are a threat to the demonic realm. These ministries are a key to seeing the church move forward and advance.

Satan hates the prophetic ministry and will attempt to block it. Prophets and prophetic people always bring fresh moves and attract revival. This is why it is so important to keep the church free from demons that hate the prophetic. Those who promote the prophetic ministry must have insight into what stops and blocks the prophetic flow.

Do you have a passion for seeing and experiencing revival and the glory of God? Do you desire to see churches filled with light and power? Do you want to see revival spread across the land? Do you desire to have the keys that unlock doors and open the way for salvation, healing, and deliverance? If your answer is yes, then I believe you have the right book in your hand. This book will challenge you to rise up and be the overcomer you are called to be.

—JOHN ECKHARDT
BEST-SELLING AUTHOR, *PRAYERS THAT ROUT DEMONS*

INTRODUCTION

WHAT IF I told you that there was a secretive conspiracy in operation, lurking just beneath the surface of your daily life and affairs? I know, you would most likely roll your eyes and say something like, "Oh no, not another crazy conspiracy theory!" I understand that the word *conspiracy* brings all kinds of emotions and thoughts, but go with me on a journey for just a moment.

When you were born again, you were re-created in the image and likeness of God. You were suddenly and powerfully brought into the world of the supernatural. There are spiritual forces at work in every element of your life. You have been given access to the realm of seeing, hearing, and knowing. Jesus said that He would send us a comforter to help and assist in our walk with God. Holy Spirit came to reside on the inside of us, providing the force and the power of the anointing of God in every area of our lives so that we become conquerors!

The anointing creates unstoppable power and momentum that bring explosive results in the kingdom of God. The devil and his minions absolutely hate the anointing. They want to shut down the flow of God's power and ability in your life.

Hell has launched a dark, malicious conspiracy against you. The word *conspire* means "to join in a secret agreement to do an unlawful or wrongful act."[1] In this book I will unmask three of hell's unlawful conspirators. I will show you how these particular spirits have similarities in their operations to bind and quench the life-giving breath and anointing of God. This evil toxic trio twists, turns, seduces, and restricts in order to hinder the spiritual progress of God's people.

However, exposure creates opportunity for deliverance! As you embark on this journey into revealing truths, your spiritual eyes will be opened to see and recognize the hidden operations of these evil spirits and the pathways of deliverance. It is time for you personally to come under the refreshing winds of heaven and be released into your new season. It is time for the heaviness to go. It is time for your destiny to manifest. It is time to see your prophetic promises realized.

I will rip the veil off the Jezebel spirit that has been at work throughout history to seduce God's people and kill the prophets. I will lay bare the evil operations of this foul anti-anointing spirit. You will see how it has robbed mankind throughout the ages and is currently at work in various facets of society. I will share personal experiences with you to arm you with strategies to overcome its power and walk free.

I will expose the python spirit with its multifaceted operations. Many people fall prey to the attack of this spirit by being ignorant of what they are actually facing. This spirit hits on various fronts to choke out the wind of God in the life of a believer. A python attack can create spiritual, emotional, and physical suffocation. Revealing this vile serpent brings tremendous liberty to the people of God. You will be fully armed to break the grip of this demon.

I will reveal to you the personal and corporate operations of the religious spirit. This spirit comes in subtly to sow legalism and bondage into the hearts of God's people. It dilutes identity and purpose to stifle the fresh prophetic revelation in the lives of believers. You will see it clearly and receive strategy to overcome it on every level.

Exposing the conspiracy tactics of this toxic trio is not just about studying these spirits—it is about setting you on course for a greater walk in the Spirit. It is about entering God's prophetic times and seasons for your life. It is about enjoying the invigorating winds of heaven. Together we will go on a journey of revelation and impartation. We will uncover, expose, bind, break, decree, and release. We will stir up the fresh winds of personal revival and forge a brave path ahead into destiny. The toxic trio will fall, and the will of heaven will be manifested in your life!

> Therefore do not fear them, for there is nothing concealed that will not be revealed, or hidden that will not be known.
> —MATTHEW 10:26, NASB

Chapter 1

THE REALITY OF
THE UNSEEN REALM

GOD TOOK ME into a vision of the future as I was ministering with a dear friend of mine who carries a strong prophetic mantle for the nation of America. We were ministering to people prophetically, laying hands on them, and releasing the word of the Lord. I walked onto the platform next to my friend, and I was immediately caught up into another dimension. It came in an instant! It was as though a whirlwind were carrying me higher and higher up into the spirit realm.

Suddenly I was swept up into this powerful encounter in the realm of the spirit. I was caught up, and God was about to show me something of great significance. This is how prophetic communication and experiences often occur in my life; they come in a moment, carrying great purpose. In a single instant God can give a message that changes the course of a person, ministry, family, or nation. We must learn to recognize, emphasize, and value these types of experiences. They carry communication from another realm.

As I was swept into the realm of the spirit, I saw the stadiums in America erupting with uncontrollable fire. The fire of deliverance was hitting the masses. It was not calm but violent in nature as the purging fires of heaven burned out demon powers. There was an intermingling of fire and glory, bringing mass deliverance. I asked the Lord about what I saw; He told me that there is a dimension of glory so heavy that it displaces demons. People can be set free in this glory.

In this vision I saw the fire of Pentecost knocking multitudes off their feet with Upper Room power. There was an extreme outpouring of fire like what fell in chapter 2 of the book of Acts. What I saw was unlike anything I ever witnessed in large gatherings. It was much more intense and radical. The Lord told me, "It is coming!"

There is a fiery move coming forth. The Lord told me this fire and glory will be carried by the pure. He is going to use those who have refused to change their message to please religious spirits. He is mantling those who have chosen not to bow to political systems in the church but have stayed tuned in to what heaven is declaring. They will operate in this next level of fire and glory.

DIMENSIONS AND VIEWPOINTS

Almost a year later I was hosting a conference where one of the great prophets in our nation was speaking. He began to weep as he shared dreams the Lord had given him for America. He shared about the move of mass deliverance he saw coming to the nation. As he poured out from his spirit, it was like lightning hit me. I heard him speak of the very same things I had seen that day when I was shown the coming move of fire.

These encounters may sound strange or unusual, but they are typical for born-again people filled with the Spirit of God. Prophetic experiences and encounters should be a daily occurrence for Christians. It should not seem strange or unusual that people are having dreams and visions of that which is and that which is to come. It was these types of supernatural encounters that fueled the move of God in the early church. As heaven spoke, the people moved.

We are living and breathing here on earth, yet we are born of another dimension, called to occupy another space. We are spiritual beings temporarily parked in this natural realm.

> Brothers, become fellow imitators with me and observe those who walk according to our example. For many are walking in such a way that they are the enemies of the cross of Christ. I have told you of them often and tell you again, even weeping. Their destination is destruction, their god is their appetite, their glory is in their shame, their minds are set on earthly things. But our citizenship is in heaven, from where also we await for our Savior, the Lord Jesus Christ, who will transform our body of humiliation, so that it may be conformed to His glorious body, according to the working of His power even to subdue all things to Himself.
>
> —PHILIPPIANS 3:17–21

Paul paints a vivid picture of people living with two drastically different perspectives. In one group the people have their minds set on earthly things, therefore missing the heavenly prize. They are so focused on this present world that their lives are void of spiritual power and significance. Paul boldly declares that this would not be his pathway, nor would it be the journey of the Philippian church. They were navigating two spaces, this present world and that which is to come. They were active and effective in living, working, and building during their time on earth, but their walk was empowered by the realization that they were effectively representing another dimension. They were heavenly citizens, ambassadors, equipped to subdue the powers of darkness, shipwreck the strategies of hell, and release the kingdom.

This is a picture of how we are to walk. We are to be representatives of the heavenly sphere with supernatural power and authority functioning in the *now*. We are not waiting for a one-day breakthrough or blessing. We are to be moving, living, working, and functioning in it right now!

There is an often unseen realm of the spirit. Many pastors and ministry leaders are facing conflict and challenge in their churches. They think they are just having difficulty with a rebellious person, but there is something deeper at work in these situations. Many families are facing sudden struggle that is so overwhelming that family members are battling the urge to leave and break up the family. Their minds are under siege, and their commitment is being tested. The devil wants to hide behind natural reasoning and human wisdom.

Let me be clear: I believe in counseling, renewing the mind, and growing in wisdom. Not every challenge can be resolved by casting out a demon. Sometimes people must work to grow in wisdom, to advance in understanding, and to change some things about themselves. We are three-part beings.

> May the very God of peace sanctify you completely. And I pray to God that your whole spirit, soul, and body be preserved blameless unto the coming of our Lord Jesus Christ.
> —1 THESSALONIANS 5:23

To be sanctified wholly, we must deal with our threefold nature. We are a spirit. The spirit part of our being contains the DNA of heaven. My spirit is not ever depressed. My spirit does not desire the nature of the enemy or lust after the works of hell. When I was born again, the kingdom came to rest in my spirit with all power and authority. If believers learned how to live and dwell in the spirit realm, they would live their lives in victorious exploits. The enemy works to bombard and overwhelm them, to trap them in the beggarly elements of earth, but God has called them to soar high above the works of darkness.

The second part of man is the soul. I believe this complex part of our being is the mind, will, and emotions. It is the part that feels, understands, and chooses. This part can become toxic without the washing of the water by the Word of God.

> That He might sanctify and cleanse it with the washing of water by the word.
>
> —Ephesians 5:26

The Word of God is like a Holy Spirit washing machine that removes the stains and pains of past experiences, turmoil, and torment. The reality of the Word of God can and will annihilate bondage in a human soul.

Healing Wounded and Damaged Souls

A wounded and damaged soul becomes a breeding ground for wrong spiritual influences. In fact, wounded emotions can act as gateways to demonic powers. The devil understands that your beliefs determine your direction. One of his warfare strategies is to infiltrate the way you think. He wants to empower false belief systems, toxic thinking, and reckless emotional upheaval.

> That you put off the former way of life in the old nature, which is corrupt according to the deceitful lusts, and be renewed in the spirit of your mind; and that you put on the new nature, which was created according to God in righteousness and true holiness.
>
> —Ephesians 4:22–24

Healing wounds in the soul is a critical step in personal freedom. It firmly closes an open door to the powers of the enemy. Here are some simple steps that serve as keys to help you dismantle emotional bondages that the enemy has constructed in your life.

Recognize the problem.

The first step to recovery is recognition. You can identify patterns, emotional outbursts (when the wound is triggered), and unhealthy cycles. Seeing that there is a problem empowers confrontation and healing. Denial empowers the bondage to remain. Many people with soul wounds live in a continual state of denial and false blame. This allows the hurt to remain and the problem to be camouflaged.

Get to the root.

You need Holy Spirit's guidance, deliverance, healing, and cleansing. Once you have recognized a problem, allow Holy Spirit to shine a bright light on the root system. How did this begin? What was the point of trauma? What is the root system that I need to deal with? For example, a wound of rejection can manifest as anger, but that is just the fruit, not the root. The healing must go down all the way to the root. The entry wound needs to be dealt with. Often this process will require assistance from other skilled ministers, depending on the depth of the issue.

Confront inner thoughts and lies.

Lies come to block the working of truth. The Word of God is truth! It is your foundation and must be the basis from which you draw your identity. Every deep emotional wound will form a series of lies that empower the existence of the wound. You must boldly confront the lies and make a decision to uproot them.

Replace lies with truth.

There is healing in the Word of God. If the enemy has planted a lie in you that says you are not valuable, then you must get Scripture that contradicts that lie. The Word acts as an antidote to the toxic infection of lies and bondage.

Meditate on the Word.

Release transformation through meditation. Meditation is the system of spiritual digestion. You must get in the truth and pray over those verses. Speak them, ponder them, and allow them to penetrate to the deepest recesses of your mind and emotions. This process draws out the healing properties of the Word of God. Sometimes you will spend days and months in the same verses because you are chewing them up and digesting them. You may need to write them and post them on the walls as reminders of your promise.

Break behavior patterns and cycles tied to lies.

Each and every wound will create bad behavior patterns and cycles. Once you have dealt with the root, you have displaced the power of the wound, but there may be residual patterns that need to be broken. If you have acted a certain way for years, it is now routine and you have to make a conscious decision not to allow that behavior anymore. When you catch yourself falling back into an old pattern, be quick to do a course correct. Sometimes, if the wound was severe, you may actually have to learn how to act normally. This is particularly true in the area of relationships.

Resist, worship, and walk it out.

Coming out of these patterns can be a process. There must be resistance on a regular basis. Worship and inviting the presence of God into your life bring oil into what can feel like a dry process. Then you must walk it out—day by day, bit by bit. Don't get discouraged if you have a thought that is not healthy— this is a temptation. Cast it down and keep pressing on. Give yourself permission to walk out the process.

Rest in the grace of God.

You must come back to the perfect work of the Cross. One of the things Jesus did was take all emotional upheaval and wounds in your place. His unfailing love and perfect work empower your freedom. You must not and cannot get trapped in condemnation and self-righteousness. Having a strong understanding of God's grace and goodness will empower your recovery.

Part of maturing in the new nature is accessing new ways of thinking. The Word of God becomes the road map to proper thinking and therefore opens the gateways to kingdom living. Once you think differently, you live differently. Renewing the mind is not a single-step process but a journey of continual change, growth, and renewal.

Here is a list of ten types of damaged souls, their symptoms, and Scripture passages to renew your mind and put you on the path toward proper thinking.

1. Conflicted soul—unable to make rational decisions, tossed to and fro, highly unstable and overly emotional

   A sound mind makes for a robust body, but runaway emotions corrode the bones.
   —PROVERBS 14:30, THE MESSAGE

2. Tormented soul—high levels of accusation, fear of punishment, dread over past mistakes, a heavy lack of peace

There is therefore now no condemnation for those who are in Christ Jesus, who walk not according to the flesh, but according to the Spirit.

—ROMANS 8:1

And the peace of God, which surpasses all understanding, will protect your hearts and minds through Christ Jesus.

—PHILIPPIANS 4:7

3. Fearful soul—fearful and anxious on a regular basis, unable to do certain activities because of abnormal levels of fear

For God has not given us the spirit of fear, but of power, and love, and self-control.

—2 TIMOTHY 1:7

There is no fear in love, but perfect love casts out fear, because fear has to do with punishment. Whoever fears is not perfect in love.

—1 JOHN 4:18

4. Anxious soul—nervous and easily panicked, void of peace and rest, anxiety attacks and bouts with a racing heart and/or heavy breathing

Be anxious for nothing, but in everything, by prayer and supplication with gratitude, make your requests known to God.

—PHILIPPIANS 4:6

5. Rejected soul—easily offended and continually needing unnatural levels of affirmation

If my father and my mother forsake me, then the LORD will take me in.

—PSALM 27:10

All whom the Father gives Me will come to Me, and he who comes to Me I will never cast out.

—JOHN 6:37

6. Weary soul—tired and frustrated, a lack of flow in the Spirit, feeling frustrated and assuming that kingdom works will not produce promised harvest

For I satiate the weary souls and I replenish every languishing soul.

—JEREMIAH 31:25

Come to Me, all you who labor and are heavily burdened, and I will give you rest. Take My yoke upon you, and learn from Me. For I am meek and lowly in heart, and you will find rest for your souls.

—MATTHEW 11:28–29

7. Offended soul—holding grudges and refusing to let go of past wrongs; this type of emotional wound is yoked to a spirit of bitterness and infirmity that can manifest in various crippling illnesses

Bear with one another and forgive one another. If anyone has a quarrel against anyone, even as Christ forgave you, so you must do.

—COLOSSIANS 3:13

Pursue peace with all men, and the holiness without which no one will see the Lord, watching diligently so that no one falls short of the grace of God, lest any root of bitterness spring up to cause trouble, and many become defiled by it.

—Hebrews 12:14–15

8. Lost soul—vagabond mentality, refusing to be established in the Word of God and the will of God

Blessed is the man who walks not in the counsel of the ungodly, nor stands in the path of sinners, nor sits in the seat of scoffers; but his delight is in the law of the Lord, and in His law he meditates day and night. He will be like a tree planted by the rivers of water, that brings forth its fruit in its season; its leaf will not wither, and whatever he does will prosper.

—Psalm 1:1–3

9. Wounded soul—enduring hurts and long-term wounds; this creates a toxic mental environment that sees everything in a negative light

The Lord is my shepherd; I shall not want. He makes me lie down in green pastures; He leads me beside still waters. He restores my soul; He leads me in paths of righteousness for His name's sake.

—Psalm 23:1–3

[The Lord] gathers together the outcasts of Israel. He heals the broken in heart, and binds up their wounds.

—Psalm 147:2–3

10. Confused soul—vacillating between ideas, unsure of identity, lacking clarity, not resolute and firm in thought, decision, or direction

The steps of a man are made firm by the LORD; He delights in his way.

—PSALM 37:23

YOUR EARTHLY HOUSE

The third part of man is the body. Your body permits you to be here on planet Earth, the house for your spirit man. Hebrews 9:27 says, "As it is appointed for men to die once, but after this comes the judgment." This verse is not referring to spiritual death but to physical death. It teaches a basic Bible doctrine that every human being will eventually experience death in the flesh and then enter eternity.

Instead, I say that we are confident and willing to be absent from the body and to be present with the Lord.

—2 CORINTHIANS 5:8

The moment our natural bodies take their final breaths, we are instantly swept into another dimension. We do not die in terms of the spiritual dimensions; we simply shift arenas. We are no longer confined by the limitations of earthly bodies but are swallowed up into the realm of the spirit to receive our eternal rewards. This is one of the reasons why we must boldly teach and preach that the spirits of the dead are not hanging around on earth. Grandma is not coming back to talk with you—it is a demon spirit that is mimicking her. She has entered the realm of eternity. No loved one who passed away is in your present; he is in your future.

The physical body has appetites that must be bridled in order to do the will of God. To have a rich and vibrant spirit life, you must conquer fleshly living.

> I say then, walk in the Spirit, and you shall not fulfill the lust of the flesh. For the flesh lusts against the Spirit, and the Spirit against the flesh. These are in opposition to one another, so that you may not do the things that you please. But if you are led by the Spirit, you are not under the law. Now the works of the flesh are revealed, which are these: adultery, sexual immorality, impurity, lewdness, idolatry, sorcery, hatred, strife, jealousy, rage, selfishness, dissensions, heresies, envy, murders, drunkenness, carousing, and the like. I warn you, as I previously warned you, that those who do such things shall not inherit the kingdom of God.
>
> —GALATIANS 5:16–21

You must learn to live from the realm of the spirit and subdue the nature of your flesh. Discipline is a key ingredient to victory. Our bodies were created to serve us; we were not created to serve our bodies. There is often a struggle between the desires of the flesh and the realm of the spirit. It is conquered by being intentional and consistent in developing the spiritual life. As you learn to live from the place of the spirit, you will override the natural appetites of the flesh.

> See then that you walk circumspectly, not as fools but as wise, redeeming the time, because the days are evil. Therefore do not be unwise, but understand what the will of the Lord is. And do not be drunk with wine, in which is dissipation; but be filled with the Spirit, speaking to one another in psalms and hymns and spiritual songs, singing and making melody in your heart to the Lord, giving thanks always for all things to God the Father in the name of our Lord Jesus Christ, submitting to one another in the fear of God.
>
> —EPHESIANS 5:15–21, NKJV

Maximizing Spiritual Moments

Paul encourages us to live rich spiritual lives, redeeming the time. He gives us a picture of maximizing moments and reaching the full spiritual intention of each season. How is this accomplished? It is reached through a daily infilling of Holy Spirit! He instructs us not to be drunk on wine but rather to be filled with the Spirit. The indication here is that there is a dwelling place in the glory of God that produces a similar effect to drunkenness.

Have you ever been in a restaurant enjoying a quiet evening, only to be interrupted by people who have had too much to drink? They forget about everyone else. They are louder, bolder, and brutally honest because they are drunk. It is the same picture that we have in the Upper Room. Newly filled disciples came staggering out of a prayer meeting and were accused by the religious of being drunk. (See Acts 2:13.) They acted and spoke differently. Their level of boldness increased. There is a realm in the spirit that produces the intoxication of heaven and fuels personal, regional, and global revival!

This is the type of radical spirit living that comes from a fresh flow of Holy Spirit power in our lives. We are no longer timid but free to be as bold as lions (Prov. 28:1). Intentional communion with Holy Spirit brings greater awareness of the realm of the spirit and supernatural living. The picture in Paul's writings is not of a single encounter but a daily walk. We are called to receive a fresh flow of heaven daily. We are called to receive heavenly wisdom, heavenly insight, and heavenly empowerment. We were *never* called to live spiritually stagnant.

The word *dwell* means "to remain for a time; to live as a resident; to keep the attention directed; to speak or write insistently."[1] This is not a picture of passive pursuit but of an intentional lifestyle. We are called to live in the dimension of the spirit. One of the schemes of hell is to cause our minds, attention, and eyes to be fixed upon the natural realm, which dilutes our spiritual sensitivity and shipwrecks our faith.

PRAYER IS A CORNERSTONE

One of the cornerstones of spirit living is prayer. At its heart, prayer is communication with God. There are many types of prayer that are valid and important. For example, the prayer of agreement is when two believers simply agree on a promise. A prayer of binding is when a child of God exercises legal authority over the works of darkness, forbidding their operation and advancements. There is a prayer of deep groaning and travail in the spirit, a gut-wrenching birthing in which the spirit dimension takes over the faculties of a believer to cry out in unknown languages and sounds until victory is realized in the spirit. A seasoned believer learns and utilizes the different facets of prayer. To engage the realm of the spirit, a person must be seasoned in prayer and active in daily fellowship with God.

> Rejoice always. Pray without ceasing. In everything give thanks, for this is the will of God in Christ Jesus concerning you. Do not quench the Spirit. Do not despise prophecies. Examine all things. Firmly hold onto what is good.
> —1 THESSALONIANS 5:16–21

These verses illustrate the lifestyle that unfolds the spirit dimension. We are instructed to "pray without ceasing." What does this look like practically? Is this stating we should neglect our family responsibilities and commitments and remain in a prayer closet 24/7? I don't believe these verses communicate that at all. I believe they are telling us that in all things we are to maintain an attitude of continual prayer. I say it like this: "Live tuned in!" We live with an ear on the heartbeat of Jesus, continually leaning in and looking into the realm of the spirit, listening, and being quick to heed His instructions.

In John Eckhardt's best-selling book *Prayers That Rout Demons* he writes, "Our source of power is the Holy Spirit and the Word of God. We build ourselves up in faith when we confess the Word of God. We experience greater confidence when we understand the Word and walk in revelation. Prayer plugs us into the power source. Prayer connects us to God and allows His power to flow to us in any situation."[2]

We were made to live in communion with God. We are called to dwell in His presence. We are marked and mantled as carriers of the glory. You can never carry the glory if you have not first heard His voice! The accuracy of hearing Him is contingent upon the strength of listening. Prayer is a two-way conversation. It is a dialogue in which you offer your heart up to God through intimate conversation and come into His presence, allowing Him to reveal His heart to you.

Every world changer has a red-hot prayer life! Prayer is the lifeblood of spiritual progress, breakthrough, and exploits. Without clear direction, intimate fellowship, and radical pursuit, there will be no supernatural displays of power.

> Confess your faults to one another and pray for one another, that you may be healed. The effective, fervent prayer of a righteous man accomplishes much. Elijah was a man subject to natural passions as we are, and he prayed earnestly that it might not rain, and it did not rain on the earth for three years and six months. And he prayed

again, and the sky gave rain, and the earth brought forth
its fruit.

—JAMES 5:16–18

The word *fervent* in James 5:16 comes from a Greek word
meaning to be active, operative, or put forth power.[3] Another
definition is "energize, working in a situation which brings it
from one stage (point) to the next, like an electrical current
energizing a wire, bringing it to a shining light bulb."[4] This type
of fervent prayer releases spiritual power that opens the heavens
and releases the strength of the kingdom. It is vital in spiritual
warfare because things are never moved in the realm of the
spirit without prayer. Prayer is the power that turns on the light
of revelation. Without prayer there is no revelation, and without
revelation there is no effective warfare.

Some time ago I was preaching and felt prompted to follow
in the footsteps of the apostle Paul. Paul prayed a powerful and
effective prayer on behalf of the church at Ephesus, as chroni-
cled in Ephesians 1. He asked that the eyes of their inner man
be opened. I prayed this prayer over a lady, and she told me that
almost immediately she became aware of the spiritual realm in
a much more profound way. (This is one of the things that apostolic people and leaders must do—release life-giving impartation and activate the spiritual sight of the church.) Her spiritual
vision surged as she became acutely aware of atmospheres, bondages, needs, and potential breakthroughs. At first she was almost
overwhelmed by all that her spiritual senses were picking up,
which is often the case when people have their spiritual senses
kicked into high gear. She shared with me the struggle that she
was having sitting in a church service when she began to see
and sense things. She lost track of what was happening in the

meeting, distracted by the tangibility of the spirit realm and all that was going on around her.

Mature prophetic people come to understand that seeing or knowing something is not an automatic release to act upon it. Once your eyes are opened, you find yourself seeing frequently because the veil between the spiritual and natural realms is torn down. Prophetic seeing and knowing must be weighed by the Word of God. They must be weighed by the spiritual authority in your life and ministry. All things in the kingdom are subject to authority. This means that if I am under another person's authority, I must be subject to his or her chain of command and protocol. Many believe that once their spiritual senses become active, it is a license to release anything at any time, but that is an extremely immature prophetic paradigm.

> Let every person be subject to the governing authorities, for there is no authority except from God, and those that exist are appointed by God. Therefore whoever resists the authority resists what God has appointed, and those who resist will incur judgment.
>
> —Romans 13:1–2

In the early church the apostles were on the front lines exposing demon rulers, confronting them, and mobilizing the church to tear them down. Paul fervently sought an impartation of insight and heavenly vision for his spiritual children. He wanted them to be keenly aware of the spirit realm. Without this awareness there is no action plan for victory. The enemy will reduce you to a realm of carnality and defeat. This is part of his strategy—to bombard your natural senses, physical desires, and emotional well-being until you become oblivious to the realm of the spirit.

Demon powers find satisfaction in the destruction of

humanity. They war against us, the children of God, because our very existence reminds them of the downtrodden and cursed place in which they have been assigned to live. They strive to kill the God nature in us and degrade our lives to a series of monotonous, carnal activities with no spiritual impact. They infiltrate our thinking with humanistic arguments and fleshly wisdom, denying the realm of the supernatural. This is a master strategy that keeps demonic entities under the cover of darkness without exposure and empowers their wicked schemes.

PROPHETIC PEOPLE

Prophets and prophetic people are like spotlights. They violently break through the murky abyss and uncloak the weapons of the enemy. James W. Goll masterfully describes these vital roles in his book *The Seer*:

> As an anointed people, we as the Body of Christ have been called to carry a prophetic-type burden that will cause us to live on the cutting edge of God's eternal purpose. The prophetic ministry is but one aspect of the five-fold calling of apostles, prophets, evangelists, pastors, and teachers. As such, it is resident to a degree in every ministry and more evident and active in certain ones. God's ultimate weapon is a man or a woman who has encountered the prophetic anointing. God does not anoint *projects*; He anoints *people*!
>
> People anointed with a prophetic ministry speak the word of the Lord in the name of the Lord. They carry weight in the Church by virtue of the ethical, moral, and spiritual urgency of their message. Their credentials, credibility, and status as prophetic vessels stem not from birth or official designation, but by the power of their inner call and by the response of those who hear them.[5]

I often say that all prophets and prophetic people live with giant targets on their backs because the forces of hell realize they can see them. The enemy cannot afford to be exposed because exposure is one of the first steps of deliverance. Without proper revelation a person, family, ministry, or region will remain firmly within the grip of demonic forces. The hidden demons must be uncovered, the plans made manifest, the attacks revealed, and the schemes divulged. This is one of the life-giving aspects of healthy prophetic ministry. Prophets and prophetic anointing shine light in the dark places and work in tandem with apostolic leaders to bring revelation that empowers building.

Learning to live with a keen sensitivity to the realm of the spirit is imperative to living a life of victory. Heaviness manifesting is often a sign of a hidden demonic power. God has provided a series of prophetic tools and spiritual gifts by which He speaks to His people. As children of God, we must educate ourselves on His methodology of speaking and be quick to recognize the message. Once we have received communication, we must effectively steward it. Learning to live with spirit eyes and ears open is key!

Prophetic power tools are given to reveal and release the will of God in the lives of people. Where the will of God is known, strength is provided. Prophecy releases power.

> But he who prophesies speaks to men for their edification
> and exhortation and comfort.
> —1 CORINTHIANS 14:3

Far too often the gifts are abused to unnecessarily wound God's people. Young and immature believers mistake what they hear and see as permission to bring accusation and manifest a spirit of rebellion.

Recently I had an encounter with a group like that. I was conducting a multiday training seminar and activating people in prophetic gifts. As time went by, I sensed an extreme heaviness hitting the room. I began to pray, and the Lord immediately highlighted 1 Corinthians 13, the love chapter. He told me to read those scriptures the following day and ask the participants to repent for any areas where they were not walking in love. He told me to have them minister to one another and let go of anything hindering them. As I obeyed the instruction of the Lord, it became obvious that there were some heavy offenses brewing in the group.

I confronted a few people and found out they were fault-finding and criticizing people in the prophetic classes. As I gave them instruction and wisdom, they had a defense for every correction. They were blinded to their own wrongdoing and walking in open rebellion. They were deceived by experiencing things they deemed spiritual; they believed they were right and everyone else was wrong, including those in authority over the seminar.

This stance violates several simple prophetic protocols, but deeper than that it opens the door for the enemy by partnering with a spirit of rebellion. If indeed they were picking up on issues with others, the first step should have been to develop the heart of an intercessor for those who were hurting. This is key to changing atmospheres and lives. God releases and reveals to bring us into a place of prayer and petition. Intercession is vital.

> For this reason we also, since the day we heard it, do not cease to pray for you and to ask that you may be filled with the knowledge of His will in all wisdom and spiritual understanding; that you may walk in a manner worthy of the Lord, pleasing to all, being fruitful in

every good work, and increasing in the knowledge of
God, strengthened with all might according to His glorious power, enduring everything with perseverance and
patience joyfully, giving thanks to the Father, who has
enabled us to be partakers in the inheritance of the saints
in light. He has delivered us from the power of darkness
and has transferred us into the kingdom of His dear Son,
in whom we have redemption through His blood, the
forgiveness of sins.

—COLOSSIANS 1:9–14

Paul was a mighty apostle of God moving in strength and
demonstration, yet he was a passionate intercessor who gave
much of his time and energy to praying for others. Intercession
is at the forefront of transformation. God will often reveal something as an invitation to pray. Prayer releases angels, strengthens
people, allows us to partner with the heavenly realm, moves
things in the heavens, and lifts people out of bondage. Prayer
releases power.

In understanding the dimensions of the spirit, we must comprehend atmospheres. The atmosphere in a place is the emotional
climate, the vibe, the feeling. Have you ever walked into a room
where people were having a heated disagreement and stopped as
soon as you walked in? Even though the verbal communication
ended, the emotional and spiritual temperature was at a boiling
point. We would say, "You could cut the tension with a knife."
That is a reference to the atmosphere. Atmospheres are manifestations of spiritual forces.

ATMOSPHERIC SHIFTS

I remember the first time I visited Disneyland. They call it a
place where dreams come true. As a small child, I had never

experienced anyplace like it. My senses were on overload. There were costumed characters everywhere. The smell of carnival foods filled the park. Every section had a theme, and even the shrubs were cut in the shapes of Disney characters. None of that happened by accident. A huge team of people worked around the clock to cultivate an atmosphere that made guests feel happy.

Just as Disneyland creates an atmosphere, churches and ministries create atmospheres. I have spoken in places where the atmosphere was so filled with hunger that you could just say the name of Jesus, and people would begin to shout! It is easy to move in the supernatural and release strong prophetic preaching in places like that because they are like spiritual wombs, alive with power and presence.

Recently this was illustrated to me in a profound way. God had given me a strong prophetic message to preach. I released it in one place with great power and authority. As I preached, it was as though layers of revelation were being released. Words, statements, and thoughts blazed across my consciousness with ease. The place erupted with shouts as I spoke. I traveled to another place and preached along the same lines, releasing the same revelation, but it felt as though every word fell flat with no impact. When I finished, I couldn't wait to leave. I felt heavy and extremely frustrated. I asked the Lord why. He told me it was the atmosphere. He said that some places have the right atmosphere to release strong prophetic insight, while others do not, as the people have not prepared themselves and the word will not be received.

When a home falls into sudden strife, it can be the manifestation of a demon spirit. When this happens, people are swept into the atmosphere of the thing without praying and discerning the source behind the heaviness. If we would be more sensitive, we would avoid a lot of unnecessary trouble. One of the most prophetic tools we have is our use of words. All of creation came into existence as a result of what God spoke in Genesis 1. We must guard and appropriate our words to create the right atmosphere and to shut the door on the wrong ones. When we announce things such as "I am in a bad mood," we are inviting in spirits of heaviness and anxiety. When we say, "I am on edge," we open the door for torment and fear. When we proclaim, "The stress is killing me," we release a two-edged attack. We empower spirits of stress, trauma, and confusion, and we also release a death decree over our bodies. Many times we say things without any thought of the consequences. These are all proclamations that shift atmospheres.

Many people just accept the current vibes in their homes as the reality without attempting to discern what is happening behind the scenes. Climates and atmospheres are typically the result of spiritual laws and principles. Atmospheres must be governed. We have authority to cleanse our homes. We can declare the promises of God, bind the forces of hell, and release the glory of God in our homes. The same principles can be applied in the workplace. I am convinced that many kingdom people are being sent into the marketplace to release and demonstrate the kingdom of God. Entire companies could shift as a result of prayer and decree!

I have seen churches and ministries suddenly come under a cloud of heaviness. This is often the result of anti-anointing spirits lurking undercover, creating false accusations, releasing division, and plundering the camp. It takes rich prophetic insight, powerful intercession, and strong apostolic authority to turn back the tide and break the attack. Powerful churches are closed today because Jezebel walked in the back door and was not discerned or dealt with. Properly discerning the spiritual climate and identifying and effectively breaking the driving force of an attack can save the life of a ministry.

POINTS TO CONSIDER

» Are you sensitive to the realm of the spirit?

» Are you aware of the atmosphere around you?

» When you sense something negative about another, do you pray or criticize?

» Have you developed regular prayer habits? If not, then when, where, and how will you start?

WHERE TO BEGIN

» Become aware of atmospheres in various places.

» Be intentional about praying over the atmospheres where you have authority.

» Pay attention to dreams, promptings, and leadings.

» Don't brush off heaviness. Ask for discernment about what is behind it, and take authority over it.

PRAYER

Father, I thank You that the eyes of my inner man are open. I thank You that I hear, see, and know in the realm of the spirit. I thank You that I do not overlook Your subtle promptings and clear directions. I ask for divine insight and spirit leading in my life. I commit my steps to You, and I will be aware of Your instructions. In Jesus's name, amen.

Chapter 2

THE POWER OF THE ANOINTING

ONE OF THE most life-giving forces in the world is the anointing of God. It is like heavenly dew and rocket fuel mixed into one. There is nothing better than teaching that is anointed, preaching that is anointed, prayers that are anointed, and atmospheres that are filled with the presence of God. When you step into a church, ministry, or meeting that is void of the anointing, it is like walking into a spiritual desert. The atmosphere is sorely lacking, and there is no sign of victory.

GOD'S POWER

In *Operating in the Anointing*, Pastor Benny Hinn writes, "Acts 1:8 promises that we will receive power after the Holy Ghost comes upon us. This promise is essential to understanding the anointing. When the Holy Spirit comes upon us, we are in God's presence. But God's presence is not the same as His anointing. God's presence is His glory and His person; His anointing is His power. In Hebrew, the word 'anoint' is *mashach*, which means 'to rub in.' The Greek word is *chrism* and means 'to smear.' When we receive the anointing, we are, in a sense, 'smeared' with His power, which means that He is not only upon us but within us, as oil would be rubbed into and absorbed by the skin. Simply put, the anointing is God's power. It is the manifestation and the result of His presence."[1]

The anointing is the power of God upon and within people to fulfill spiritual assignments, break oppression, and catapult people into destiny. God never calls someone to do something without providing an anointing! We are completely unable to do the works of Jesus, move in the supernatural, or achieve exploits without Holy Ghost power.

When the anointing hits a person or a gathering, there is a divine charge! Explosive spiritual shock waves are released, and things far beyond human achievement are accomplished. It is imperative that believers learn to value and recognize the anointing. The reality is that we are crippled in the realm of the supernatural if we do not move in the anointing.

The anointing is always connected to purpose. Prophets are anointed to prophesy and reveal. Apostles are anointed to break through, build, guide, and govern. Evangelists are anointed to work miracles and impact nations. Intercessors are anointed to pray fiery prayers that shake the heavens. Pastors are anointed to love, lead, and feed sheep. For every mandate, there is divine ability.

> You shall take the garments and clothe Aaron with the tunic and the robe of the ephod and the ephod and the breastplate, and gird him with the skillfully woven band of the ephod. And you shall put the turban on his head and put the holy crown on the turban. Then shall you take the anointing oil and pour it on his head and anoint him. You shall bring his sons and put tunics on them. You shall gird them with sashes, Aaron and his sons, and put the headbands on them, and the priest's office shall

be theirs for a perpetual statute. Thus you shall consecrate Aaron and his sons.

—Exodus 29:5–9

The Lord gave very strong instructions concerning the priest-
hood. They had to be set apart, clothed, and then anointed
to fulfill their priestly duties. This, of course, was an Old
Testament example. Under the old covenant everything manifested through type and shadow. We see things in a picture,
because God was not indwelling people as He is in our day.

> You also, as living stones, are being built up into a spiritual
> house as a holy priesthood to offer up spiritual sacrifices
> that are acceptable to God through Jesus Christ.
>
> —1 Peter 2:5

We are called priests to be set apart for the Lord. When we
become followers of Jesus, there is a full surrender. It is one of
the key elements of living a life full of spiritual power. Holy
Spirit leads us into a deeper and more intense relationship with
the Father.

What kind of clothing do we wear in the spirit? What are
our priestly garments? Are they outward or spiritual? Many in
the church debate what you can and cannot wear as children of
God. Fashion has radically changed and evolved through the
generations. While I believe in decency, the need for a person
to dictate what others should look like often comes from strong
roots in a religious mentality of bondage. I believe our priestly
garments are not natural but spiritual. We are given powerful weapons of war and armor that thwart the attacks of the
wicked one.

Finally, my brothers, be strong in the Lord and in the power of His might. Put on the whole armor of God that you may be able to stand against the schemes of the devil.

—EPHESIANS 6:10–11

In the spirit realm we have mantles, or supernatural garments, that bring life, power, and authority according to our unique assignments. We have garments of righteousness through our acceptance of the full work of Jesus at Calvary. We have spiritual armor to protect and equip us for battle.

Our anointing is not natural. It is not just oil from a bottle but divine oil from heaven filled with life, strength, and breakthrough. We all have a unique and powerful anointing available to us according to our assignments.

I will never forget one of my early experiences with the anointing. I was in Bible college and so hungry for God! I spent hours in private worship and prayer. I so desperately wanted His presence. It was as if I were in a Holy Ghost washing machine. He was powerfully cleansing and delivering me.

I had decided to join a student choir, and we were scheduled to sing at an area church. I was asked to do something special during the program, and I felt completely unqualified. I told my leader I did not feel ready. I told him I didn't have the skill to do it, and that was the truth! I did not realize it was a God setup.

As my time approached, my stomach was tied in knots. My mind was swirling; I just knew I would mess up. I got up to do my part, and sure enough, I began to mess up. Then something shifted. I felt something like liquid fire bursting forth from deep inside of me and surging from my head to my toes. It was an indescribable sensation. It was as if in a moment every high point I had ever experienced in prayer suddenly merged to become one overwhelming moment in the spirit.

Suddenly words started flowing from another realm. What was happening? What was I saying? Would I get in trouble? I was off the plan and off course, but I was in another realm. My eyes were closed, and I was saying what was coming to my spirit supernaturally, with no fear. All nervousness and fear were swallowed up in this heavenly surge.

When I finished speaking, I opened my eyes, and the altar was filled with people. Some were weeping; others, kneeling; but all were encountering God and His transforming power. The whole event switched gears and became a spontaneous revival meeting as God poured out on His people. That was the night I was totally transformed as I got a taste of both my mantle and the anointing that would catapult me into nations. The breaker showed up that night to tear down walls, remove bondages, and liberate hearts. My fears, shortcomings, and own thoughts were effortlessly swallowed up in the anointing. That was the first of many such experiences in the school of the spirit that God used to train me.

DIFFERENT FLOWS OF ANOINTING AVAILABLE TO BELIEVERS

Wherever there is anointing, there is divine flow! To accomplish the will of God, there is a need for various types of anointings. Let's explore a few anointings that need to be active in the church and in the lives of God's people.

Miracle anointing

Miracles are instant turnarounds! They are manifestations of the supernatural in everyday life. Miracles can happen in every arena of life. We can experience financial, family, debt-cancellation, and healing miracles. God is a miracle-working God! Miracles are commonplace in the kingdom of God. The miracle anointing is the divine flow of God to perform miracles. It must be recognized and maximized. Typically there are instructions from God that open up this realm of anointing.

> God worked powerful miracles by the hands of Paul. So handkerchiefs or aprons he had touched were brought to the sick, and the diseases left them, and the evil spirits went out of them.
>
> —ACTS 19:11–12

Healing anointing

Healing is one of the works Jesus accomplished on the cross. The Bible tells us He sent His word and healed us (Ps. 107:20). The healing anointing is the divine presence of God to accomplish supernatural healing. Healing can be a process. It is not unusual for someone to have a sense of strength come into his or her physical body and begin driving out the weakness.

> Now when the sun was setting, all those who had anyone sick with various diseases brought them to Him. And He laid His hands on every one of them and healed them.
>
> —LUKE 4:40

Prophetic anointing

The prophetic anointing is the power of God to prophesy, see in the spirit, receive revelation, and function prophetically. There are multiple ways that God speaks prophetically. When there is a prophetic anointing, the level of revelation and divine insight becomes explosive. When Saul came into the company of prophets, it caused the prophetic anointing to hit him, and he began to speak prophetically. That is what happens when a prophetic anointing is at work. It becomes easy to see, know, hear, and declare. Oil of revelation begins to flow from heaven.

> When they came to the hill, a group of prophets met him.
> And the Spirit of God came upon him, and he prophesied
> among them. So when all who previously knew him saw
> that he prophesied among the prophets, the people said
> one to another, "What is this that has come upon the son
> of Kish? Is Saul also among the prophets?"
>
> —1 SAMUEL 10:10–11

Financial anointing

There is a realm in the anointing that attracts increase; it
helps create wealth and tap into the abundant blessings of God.
When it is an anointing, there is an uncommon ease. Things
happen suddenly and supernaturally. Many believers miss this
realm because they do not understand that there is power
(anointing) to get wealth!

> But you must remember the LORD your God, for it is He
> who gives you the ability to get wealth, so that He may
> establish His covenant which He swore to your fathers,
> as it is today.
>
> —DEUTERONOMY 8:18

Building anointing

Throughout Scripture God places value upon building. David
told his son that he would inherit the task of building God a
magnificent house.

> Then David called Solomon his son and commanded him
> to build a house for the LORD, the God of Israel.
>
> —1 CHRONICLES 22:6

The Lord revealed Himself in this passage as the founder and
builder of the church:

> And I tell you that you are Peter, and on this rock I will
> build My church, and the gates of Hades shall not prevail
> against it.
>
> —MATTHEW 16:18

He also sent Holy Spirit to live in us and pray through us. Praying in the Spirit builds up our spirit man and the realm of faith in us. The gift of prophecy builds people up. When the word of the Lord is released, the people of God are strengthened, encouraged, and established.

God is into building, and He has provided a strong grace to build. Apostles are foundational gifts to the church. They are sent ones—sent to build! The church is called to be an advancing, prevailing, and building people. When He tells people to do particular exploits, there is divine ability to build. Leaders need to tap into the building anointing. Businesspeople need to tap the building anointing. Apostles and prophets are called to help build—they need to flow in that grace, claim it, and stir it up.

Prayer anointing

I was preaching a revival meeting when suddenly strong intercession broke out all over the building. People began to run to the altar, praying under a supernatural leading from heaven. I didn't urge it or create it; heaven just showed up and people began to move into deep realms of prayer. Whether it is in our personal lives or as a body of believers, there is an anointing for prayer that we can tap into. We should look for that river and dive deep into it!

> Even them I will bring to My holy mountain and make
> them joyful in My house of prayer.... For My house shall
> be called a house of prayer for all people.
>
> —Isaiah 56:7

Leadership anointing

Leadership—people placed in roles of authority—is a heavenly concept. Many people struggle with this because of ignorance and rebellion, but it is still the truth. God never appoints a leader without the anointing to serve. Leaders need to learn the value of the anointing in this area and make a conscious effort to ask God for it and maximize it. The people who are being served by a leader need to pray and ask the Lord to anoint the leader.

> Let every person be subject to the governing authorities,
> for there is no authority except from God, and those that
> exist are appointed by God. Therefore whoever resists the
> authority resists what God has appointed, and those who
> resist will incur judgment.
>
> —Romans 13:1–2

Helps and service anointing

Helps is listed among the supernatural ministry gifts in 1 Corinthians 12:28. There is an anointing to help. Every purpose of God, work of God, leader, and ministry needs help. There is a blessing in helping. Many churches and ministries need to pray and teach on the anointing to help. People's lives can be supernaturally changed when they begin to serve the works of the Lord.

> As everyone has received a gift, even so serve one another
> with it, as good stewards of the manifold grace of God.
>
> —1 Peter 4:10

Sonship anointing

There is an anointing for us to function as sons and daughters of God. We were once orphans, but the power of the blood of Jesus brought us into total freedom and established us in the family of God. The enemy will attempt to bring accusation and heaviness, but we do not have to receive it. We can rest in what heaven has already said and enjoy the freedom of sonship.

> Yet to all who received Him, He gave the power to become sons of God, to those who believed in His name, who were born not of blood, nor of the will of the flesh, nor of the will of man, but of God.
>
> —John 1:12–13

> Blessed be the God and Father of our Lord Jesus Christ, who has blessed us with every spiritual blessing in the heavenly places in Christ, just as He chose us in Him before the foundation of the world, to be holy and blameless before Him in love; He predestined us to adoption as sons to Himself through Jesus Christ according to the good pleasure of His will.
>
> —Ephesians 1:3–5

Family anointing

There is divine power and assistance to raise families. There is supernatural ability for marriage and relationships. Too many people only see certain things as anointed, but every covenant carries an anointing. We can tap into the realm of God's power for our families. God can teach us how to be better spouses and parents through the anointing. This is one facet of the anointing—to release revelation and insight.

But from the beginning of the creation, God "made them male and female." "For this cause shall a man leave his father and mother, and cleave to his wife, and the two shall be one flesh." So then they are no longer two, but one flesh. What therefore God has joined together, let not man put asunder.

—MARK 10:6–9

Musical anointing

Music is deeply spiritual. It can open realms and create atmospheres. A simple lyric becomes lodged in our brains for days. A certain rhythm causes our bodies to move without thinking about it. Music carries something that affects us profoundly. There is an anointing for the right kind of music. There is an anointing on songs, lyrics, and sounds. There are realms of worship that push back the powers of hell and open the heavens. We need anointed musicians, minstrels, and psalmists!

It happened that when the evil spirit from God came on Saul, David would take the lyre in his hand and play. So Saul was refreshed and was well, and the evil spirit departed from him.

—1 SAMUEL 16:23

King David raised up an army of full-time worshippers that included four thousand musicians. He said:

Four thousand shall offer praises to the LORD with the instruments that I have made for praise.

—1 CHRONICLES 23:5

Worship was a weapon of choice in Israel. It was radical worship that propelled David into the palace. He was a prophetic worshipper who knew how to tap into the anointing to push back darkness. He created an army of prophetic worshippers who staffed a throne room type of prayer-and-worship model in his kingdom. This is a model that is still relevant today. David valued the call to radical worship, prayer, and intercession. He established his own company of worship leaders who kept the incense of prayer and longing rising up to the throne of God.

> These are the singers, heads of the fathers' houses of the Levites, who lodged in the chambers, and were free from other duties; for they were employed in that work day and night.
>
> —1 Chronicles 9:33, nkjv

Deliverance anointing

One of the most elementary aspects of the anointing is the bondage-breaking power. Demon spirits entangle and ensnare, but the anointing can destroy those ties! When the anointing of God begins to move, it breaks the cords that have held God's people. There is power to set the captives free.

> The Spirit of the Lord God is upon me because the Lord has anointed me to preach good news to the poor; He has sent me to heal the broken-hearted, to proclaim liberty to the captives, and the opening of the prison to those who are bound.
>
> —Isaiah 61:1

> He said to them, "I saw Satan as lightning fall from heaven. Look, I give you authority to trample on serpents and scorpions, and over all the power of the enemy. And nothing shall by any means hurt you."
>
> —Luke 10:18–19

Regional anointing

There is an anointing to impact regions. This is one of the cornerstones of an apostolic ministry. There is an established sphere of influence. There are regional plans, regional purposes, and supernatural power to establish the kingdom of God within regions.

> We are not boasting of things beyond our measure in other men's labors. But we have hope that when your faith is increased, our region shall be greatly enlarged by you, to preach the gospel in the regions beyond you and not to boast in another man's accomplishments.
> —2 CORINTHIANS 10:15–16

Global anointing

Some have an anointing for global exploits. Their platform is the world, and they are called to go forth, shaking nations. There are global prophets who are given mandates for nations. They speak in a higher dimension of authority and insight. They are releasing prophetic insight not just for people but for nations. There are evangelists who have been supernaturally propelled forth into the nations of the world. They have faith, a word, and favor for nations. There are apostles who have been given a global platform to transform nations. They are given strong words for the nations accompanied by an earth-shaking anointing. God sends them with supernatural power and authority.

> Before I formed you in the womb I knew you; and before you were born I sanctified you, and I ordained you a prophet to the nations.
> —JEREMIAH 1:5

Corporate anointing

There is an anointing that is unique and different when God's people gather. It is the fruit of various gifts coming together under one united banner. As believers worship, pray, and pursue heaven together, there is precious dew that flows down, bringing life, strength, and breakthrough. In many ways it is a multiplication of the individual anointing upon the lives of people.

> Behold, how good and how pleasant it is for brothers to dwell together in unity! It is like precious oil upon the head, that runs down on the beard—even Aaron's beard—and going down to the collar of his garments; as the dew of Hermon, that descends upon the mountains of Zion, for there the LORD has commanded the blessing, even life forever.
>
> —PSALM 133:1–3

Believer's anointing

There is a well that dwells on the inside of every believer. It is part of our new nature and the complete work of Jesus at Calvary. We are not only appointed for dynamic kingdom works but anointed for them also. The realm of healing, miracles, casting out demons, spirit leading, and divine insight is available in the life of every believer. This has nothing to do with an office or the grace available for that specific work. This is the fruit of the kingdom in our lives. We can tap into the believer's anointing to be a powerful witness to the world and help change the lives of those around us.

> He said to them, "Go into all the world, and preach the gospel to every creature. He who believes and is baptized will be saved. But he who does not believe will be condemned. These signs will accompany those who believe: In My name they will cast out demons; they will speak

with new tongues; they will take up serpents; if they
drink any deadly thing, it will not hurt them; they will
lay hands on the sick, and they will recover."

—MARK 16:15–18

THE SECRET IS IN THE SURRENDER

God anointed Jesus of Nazareth with the Holy Spirit and
with power, who went about doing good and healing all
who were oppressed by the devil, for God was with Him.

—ACTS 10:38

Jesus walked in a tangible anointing that had maximum
impact everywhere He went. How did He maintain such a high
level of spiritual operation? The secret is in the surrender! He
was completely surrendered to the will of the Father—clinging
to His voice for instruction, continually listening, looking, and
leaning into the realm of the spirit.

For I came down from heaven, not to do My own will,
but the will of Him who sent Me.

—JOHN 6:38

Jesus was not doing His own thing. The devil did his own
thing and was swiftly kicked out of heaven. Many people follow
in the footsteps of Lucifer, seeking to live their own lives, fulfill their own dreams, build their own ministries, and compete
for their own voices to be heard. This is the epitome of demonic
behavior. There are many in the ministry who are camouflaged
rebels. They have the right language, yet they lack the surrender.

And He said to them, "I was watching Satan fall from
heaven like lightning."

—LUKE 10:18, NASB

Don't get me wrong—it is fantastic to have big, bold dreams and wild adventures of faith. I do not believe God created any human to live a boring and mundane life. Anointed people go big! The difference is the surrender. Are we allowing God to dream enormous dreams through us? Are we allowing the Father to place His desires in our hearts? Are we willing to change course at a moment's notice if the Lord asks us to? These are all questions we must ask if we dare to do exploits.

God is the ultimate dreamer and master planner. He left absolutely nothing to chance and authored every step of your destiny. He meticulously planned your entrance, your life, and your graduation from the earth realm into glory. He has ordained exploits beyond your wildest imagination.

There are too many people crouched in the corner, shackled with the bonds of disappointment. They have checked out of dreaming and are living on autopilot, merely existing. God wants to heal the dream nature inside of them. He wants to touch the broken places and command the dead bones to live again. He wants to speak to the broken dreams and declare purpose in the midst of pain.

Some had a false start. They launched into a thing without the proper timing. The Bible declares that every purpose has an appointed time (Eccles. 3:1). They heard a word, dreamed a dream, saw a vision, and stepped out with little or no thought about the timing and the plan. There is always divine timing. It is an illegal spiritual operation to advance into a thing without obtaining the wisdom of God for the timing.

Anointed people are sensitive to times and seasons. They have a strong Holy Ghost GPS. They know the dangers of a false start. Don't misunderstand me—everyone has missed it in the area of timing. Peter is perhaps one of the greatest biblical examples of a passionate disciple who kept making false starts. His passion would often get ahead of his character, yet God kept restoring him and reviving him.

I hear the Lord saying, "For every false start there is an authentic launch. Some moved before the time and received flattering words, only to be greatly disappointed, but I am binding up their wounds and reviving them. I am reigniting the fire of destiny within them. I am relaunching them for the next phase. The time shall be redeemed. The enemy has been screaming, 'It's over,' but I am saying it is just beginning!"

I see some relaunches on the horizon. It is time to launch again with fresh purpose. There is a new beginning for you. There are things to be set in motion in your life and destiny. The devil keeps intimidating you and telling you that it is over, but God is going to launch you once again with renewed passion, purpose, and momentum.

Surrender is the secret weapon of anointed people. The anointing flowing in abundance is the confirmation of surrender. Jesus was not striving to be anointed. He was doing the will of the One who sent Him. The lower He went in His own ambitions, the higher He rose in the spirit. This is a great mystery, but it is a power secret of anointed people—first is last, and last is first (Matt. 20:16).

Why is surrender so significant? Because all covenants center on sacrifice and surrender. Every covenant demands a shedding of blood. It is one of the signs of the surrender. There must be a sacrifice in order to have a legitimate covenant.

> And not through the blood of goats and calves, but through His own blood, He entered the holy place once for all, having obtained eternal redemption.
>
> —HEBREWS 9:12, NASB

COVENANT VIRTUE

Each covenant offers certain unique rights and privileges. It also creates boundaries and alliances. One of the strongest pictures of covenant thinking is in the life of Abraham. After walking through the blood, the Lord declares to Abraham that He will place a generational blessing upon his lineage (his seed). (See Genesis 15.) The obedience of Abraham and his friendship with God would have generational implications.

All too often ministers spend hours focusing on every possible generational curse, the need for repentance, and the possibility of bondage without ever emphasizing the power of a covenant with God and the generational blessings available. I believe that God is establishing strong emphasis on engaging the realm of the spirit with a covenant mind-set—in other words, stepping into a battle from a place of victory and absolutely gutting the powers of hell with the name, the Word, and the blood. If God's people awaken to their true identity and the strength of their covenant, they will be undefeatable, unstoppable, and immovable!

The Lord used strong covenant language with Abraham that makes many in the modern Christian world uncomfortable.

> I will bless them who bless you and curse him who curses
> you, and in you all families of the earth will be blessed.
> —GENESIS 12:3

This is a lost reality; nonetheless it is a spiritual law. Two people in covenant fight the same battles and share the same enemies. This is the bedrock of effective spiritual warfare. Many people have passive spirits. They want to remain neutral in every matter and avoid conflict at all costs. They create covenant alignments to get the perks yet are unwilling to defend those they are supposed to be aligned with or fight the battles with them. This is a transaction mentality and not a covenant mentality. Transactional people enter relationships to get a benefit, but they lack commitment and endurance. They are fair-weather friends and leaders who run at the first sign of trouble.

Many churches, ministries, and organizations are weak and spiritually diluted because of this false thinking. People come and go with no commitment and no covenant. These people abandon their posts at the first sign of battle. All covenants are proved in the thick of battle. When war erupts, the covenant is tested.

Let's expand our grasp on these concepts. In today's church culture we are adamant about creating converts. We send out teams to pray with people on the streets in hopes of converting them. We plan big events to draw in the lost; we design the whole thing to talk them out of going to hell and accepting Jesus. I applaud all these efforts and cheer them on—yet there is more!

Was the church instructed to simply make converts? Is this the highest expression of *ekklesia* (the church)? Should this be the ultimate aim of the church?

> Go therefore and make disciples of all the nations, baptizing them in the name of the Father and of the Son and of the Holy Spirit, teaching them to observe all things I have commanded you. And remember, I am with you always, even to the end of the age.
> —MATTHEW 28:19–20

Imagine a groom going from place to place, having numerous wedding ceremonies with different women, leaving suddenly from each, and moving to the next bride. This seems crazy, but in many ways it is what we are doing in modern Christianity. We ask people to wear the ring without fully engaging in the covenant. Conversion is only the beginning of the matter. The highest expression of the kingdom is disciples who are reproducing, representing, and establishing kingdom culture.

> It was at this time that He went off to the mountain to pray, and He spent the whole night in prayer to God. And when day came, He called His disciples to Him and chose twelve of them, whom He also named as apostles.
>
> —LUKE 6:12–13, NASB

Something was so deep in the heart of Jesus that He was up all night praying, pondering, and seeking wisdom. What could be that important? What could be that serious? He was about to choose the twelve men whom He would pour into day and night, the twelve who would change the world. He was about to select a ragtag group of men to cut a covenant with and share the deepest part of Himself. These were not casual relationships—these were the very foundations of the ministry of the Lord of glory! He was going to choose His disciples, and there was no matter deeper in the heart of Jesus than this one.

These men would eat, travel, dream, and weep together; they would fight for one another, fight against one another, and do mind-blowing exploits. Jesus began a discipleship ministry, and relationship with these men was one of His most demanding tasks. Yet His limited time with these men built the foundations of Christianity as we know it.

Jesus preached to the masses, healed the multitudes, and shook cities and regions. He spent countless hours teaching the deep things of the kingdom. He taught the unlearned using pictures, parables, and stories. But when the crowds left, He was making disciples. He was building covenant relationships and investing His very person into those men destined to change the world.

Often in this world we strive for bigger and better. We measure ourselves by our achievements, and we feel absolutely defeated if someone next to us seems to be outdoing us. Sometimes we live our whole lives doing outrageous things but never experience true covenant relationships.

Covenant places boundaries upon our lives. When we become disciples, we become surrendered ones. I am often asked what I think about particular social issues and evolving morality in our society. In the past I have been far too quick to state an opinion. I have come to understand that as I am a bondservant of Jesus, my opinion does not matter in such affairs. When I became a disciple, I became tied to the value system of heaven. I am not allowed the freedom to decide what I think is right and wrong. I have divine guidance. At times the integrity of Jesus challenges my human heart and understanding, but it is my covenant responsibility to uphold the values of Jesus. There are things that I don't do because heaven has not authorized them. A life of purpose is a life of focus and surrender.

The anointing was one of the primary things that made a difference in Jesus's ministry. As He walked the face of the earth, the tangible touch of God was upon Him. Those with issues were drawn to Him in a supernatural way. The sick, the tormented, the afflicted, and the bound came. Not only did they come, but they left forever changed.

Jesus was anointed. He was supernaturally charged to break the back of demon powers and bring miraculous results. This is one of the pillars of purpose in the anointing. The anointing provides supernatural power to break the works of hell.

> And it shall come to pass in that day, that his burden shall be taken away from off thy shoulder, and his yoke from off thy neck, and the yoke shall be destroyed because of the anointing.
>
> —Isaiah 10:27, kjv

A yoke is a piece of equipment used to connect oxen to a plow. The spiritual picture here is an instrument that attaches a person to a heavy burden. When the anointing comes, it breaks and destroys not only the evil weight but also every device that connects a person to it. Wherever there is great anointing, there is great freedom!

> Now the Lord is the Spirit. And where the Spirit of the Lord is, there is liberty.
>
> —2 Corinthians 3:17

Philip the evangelist was leading a tremendous revival. As the anointing was moving, demons were fleeing.

> When the crowds heard Philip and saw the miracles which he did, they listened in unity to what he said. For unclean spirits, crying with a loud voice, came out of many who were possessed. And many who were paralyzed or lame were healed. So there was much joy in that city.
>
> —Acts 8:6–8

Philip was leading a tremendous move of God with mass deliverance. There is nothing like a heaven-sent revival. Historically revival has been used to change the destiny of a generation and call people back into deep intimacy with God. There have been various types of revivals, but all have featured spectacular displays of God's power. There is something about miracles, signs, and wonders that pierces the hearts of people.

AN EMAIL LEADS TO REVIVAL

A strong wave of revival can overturn a church, a community, a state, or even a nation. The wave comes in like a flood, subduing the powers of hell and releasing the reality of the glorious kingdom of God. I remember a very special revival in which I was privileged to have a role. The Lord sent the pastor of a small church into my life through an email. At the time, I was leading a regional ministry, and we had regular gatherings to stoke the fires of revival. This pastor felt tugged by the Lord to reach out to me. He sent me an email stating that he knew he was supposed to connect with me, and the Lord told him that his city would be changed when I came there. As I read the words, I felt a bit overwhelmed and questioned their authenticity. After all, maybe he was just exaggerating.

This pastor began attending some of my meetings, and the Lord connected us through a series of events. We built a relationship, ministered alongside one another, and strategized about the coming days. After a long period of time, the Lord reminded me of his initial email—it was about me coming into his region. We had preached, traveled, and prayed together, but I had not yet been to his region. I felt a quickening to go. I went for what was supposed to be a weekend of meetings, but heaven swept into the building, and the miraculous of God began to break forth. There were many miracles. I vividly recall one that would become a catalyst for revival. There was an older man who said he had extreme bone problems. He had evident mobility issues and was unable to walk without major assistance. He had two canes and could barely move. As I stood before him praying, the gift of faith hit me, and I began to command him to rise up and walk. God's power overcame him, and he immediately jumped up and took off walking, completely without issue. It was a phenomenal sight. He lifted up the two canes and held them high as he walked with full mobility. Revival had begun!

I stayed in that region for months, praying, preaching, prophesying, and holding revival meetings alongside the host pastor. There were many prophetic confirmations about what God was doing. The Lord had sent many other trailblazers ahead to seed the ground with the Word of the Lord. People began to come from various states and regions, and we outgrew the small church where the meetings began and had to rent a larger facility. Everything was supernatural! People were healed, saved, and filled with Holy Spirit. Lives were forever changed, and kingdom plans were birthed.

In a "suddenly" moment God fulfilled words given years before over that pastor, his church, and the region. He partnered with prophetic words given years before about the name of and strategy for this move. The Lord grew his ministry far beyond what it was when the revival began.

This is one of the reasons why demon spirits hate revival. Revival can bring a sudden fulfillment of dormant promises. Revival releases tremendous velocity in the spirit that breaks the clutch of demons. Revival can refresh the driest people and penetrate the hardest hearts. Revival releases a torrent of anointing and glory that plunders the structures of hell. The devil hates revival and strives to attack any person or ministry pressing in for it.

The anointing obliterates demonic powers. This is why there are demon spirits that have an assignment against the anointing. They want to quench the fresh flow of heaven in ministries, believers, and worship times. They want to stifle and bind up men and women of God. They want to create dry, dead, religious atmospheres that pose no threat to their kingdom. They launch strategic attacks against the people of God and against anointed places. They do not strike randomly but with intent.

These demons are called anti-anointing spirits. They fight and hinder the flow of life and power in the realm of the spirit. In 1 John 2:18 there is a warning about antichrists: "Little children, it is the last hour. As you have heard that the antichrist will come, even now there are many antichrists. By this we know that it is the last hour." What is the meaning of *antichrists*? *Christ* represents the Anointed One and His anointing. So the picture here is of a family of demonic entities that have a target to fight the anointing. They are on assignment to subdue, restrict, and overwhelm.

When a ministry begins bringing in a fresh anointing of life and power, these antichrist spirits take notice and conceive heinous plans to stop the flow. They will send strife, division, accusation, hindrance, and financial attacks. They launch an all-out assault to stop the flow.

As we expound on the toxic trio of demons in this book, we will identify their operations and expose their agenda. While each of the three spirits is unique, they are similar in their type. They are all spirits that work to destroy the anointing of God.

POINTS TO CONSIDER

» Have you experienced resistance when you have pressed in to particular spiritual assignments?

» Your anointing is connected to your purpose.

» Resistance is confirmation that what you are doing is dangerous to the kingdom of darkness.

» What areas of your life need to be surrendered?

» What is the Lord dealing with you about concerning devotion, obedience, and surrender?

WHERE TO BEGIN

» Learn to recognize spiritual resistance in your personal life, ministry assignments, and corporate body of believers.

» Bind the enemy when you sense the resistance.

» Tap into the various types of anointings that are available for your life. Pray over them—confess that they are yours, and ponder the scriptures associated with them.

PRAYER

Father, I thank You that I am created for a purpose and destined for kingdom assignments. I ask You to help me recognize the resistance of the enemy and be strong in You to break the powers of darkness. I confess that I am fully committed to kingdom assignments, mandates, and relationships. I am spiritually sensitive, activated, and aware, in Jesus's name.

Chapter 3

JEZEBEL, THE SPIRITUAL ASSASSIN

I WAS A YOUNG ministry pioneer embarking on a brand-new adventure. God had given me direction, and I was ready to go. I could not wait to fulfill the dreams that were in my heart. My sense of expectation was surging as I stepped forward to answer the call to birth something new. It was a faith adventure in every way. I felt the Lord leading me into unknown territory with few resources. I had a word, I had a dream, and I had faith—with that I jumped into the deep and launched a brand-new ministry.

SHE WANTS THE HEADS OF FORERUNNERS

In the early stages of the journey the Lord brought someone before me whom I had only casually met a few times through some ministry friends. I felt as though I was in over my head, trying to launch something with no help. I reached out to that casual acquaintance to see if there was any interest in joining our ragtag team and launching into the deep. To my surprise, the answer was yes! We added a new team member.

As our team grew, there were exciting new relationships. People were being added to assist in the various areas, and God was doing all types of miracles. We experienced financial miracles, healing miracles, family miracles, and strong waves of deliverance. Our meetings were always unique. God showed up in power each and every time.

Two of the team members were a gracious couple who seemed to have a strong hospitality gifting and to be ready to serve in any way. As time progressed, I had some subtle checks but nothing too drastic. There were some questions, little concerns, things that I would find a way to brush off because I felt as though I needed every helper I could get. What would we do if we lost a key person?

One night while alone with this couple, I witnessed something that startled me and shook my confidence. The wife began to have a conversation with a member of my family that seemed to take a "prophetic" turn, probing into past wounds and pains. It happened suddenly and without warning. There were some accurate details and pieces of information, but as it unfolded, I knew in my spirit something was terribly off. What was it?

The event had some of the markings of a prophetic encounter, but there was something underlying. It was forceful, was obtrusive, and ended in confusion with no peace. Even deeper, when it was unfolding, there was not an awareness of God's love and redemptive nature. There was instead a sense of unlawful operation. There was a spiritual dynamic taking place, but it wasn't at all good or comforting. I knew that something was terribly amiss, and I knew that I would never allow anything like that again on my team. Now I had to discern what was taking place.

I maintained a heart of pursuit with an attitude of seeking wisdom to resolve what I was sensing. Soon it would all play out in vivid detail. There was an underlying agenda with a power play that would unfold. What I sensed during that encounter was far greater than what I knew at that time. I was about to have a battle with a spirit that I had encountered before. This would be one of the first of many rounds with this spirit in that phase of my life and ministry. The same demonic entity would show up again and again with a determination to shut down our ministry and back me into a corner. It tried, but it did not prevail.

As time passed, there were further confirmations of the suspicions we had about the couple on our team. One of the most vivid skirmishes was when this spirit confronted me and my wife late one night in the couple's home. It was an actual spirit that showed up and began to unload a massive attack. We both sensed the evil presence, and our minds started to swirl as the demon unloaded garbage and accusation. I knew in that moment that there was an unclean nature to the spirit in that home. It had an assignment of seduction. I would come to find out that seduction is one of the primary tools of the devil that we were about to confront.

The entire thing came to a head after a series of small rebellions. The couple would choose to ignore an instruction, to do something they were not permitted to do, or to take charge of a corporate gathering without my permission. The once seemingly kind and loving couple morphed into something very different. There were major emotional and spiritual instabilities manifesting in the wife. The husband seemed firm at times but uncommonly passive at other times. There was something about the wife that appeared lustful but remained cloaked under a stream of "God said" statements, kind acts, and prophetic declarations.

Finally there was an ultimatum delivered. I was told that the word of the Lord had been given that the wife was supposed to be my co-leader. The Lord had spoken to her that she was not to be under my authority but on an equal playing field. There was much pressure given to make the case, and her husband dutifully went along with it. Eventually we were in a state of strong disagreement, and a power play was under way. It was only after I discerned what was glaringly apparent behind the scenes that the full extent of the spiritual force was revealed—this was a wrestling for control, illegal access, and illegitimate authority. This was a power play by the Jezebel spirit.

I could now clearly see the roles of Ahab and Jezebel in this scenario. I want to be clear that this spirit can and will operate through any gender. It is simply looking for a host to seduce, control, and manifest through. I drew a firm line in the sand and stood up to the spirit. There was only one choice: repent and be free, or exit the team. After much posturing, attempted manipulation, and exaggerated emotions, the couple exited. This was the first of many battles we had in that ministry with that particular spirit.

WARRIORS WIN!

Through the years, I have often been criticized for my preaching on demons and the Jezebel spirit, in particular. Many times I have wished that I wouldn't have to see, hear, or deal with these wicked enemies. I wish that I could live as others do, like ostriches with their heads in the sand, but I cannot. I am a warrior! I am a justice person who sees things as absolute. I hate the devil and the powers of hell. I cannot afford to be passive in spiritual warfare, or the enemy will take me out. *You* cannot afford to be passive either.

My education on the Jezebel spirit was born in the belly of the fight. I never intended to learn about or preach on this spirit, but I fought it many times, as will any prophetic person. It is one of the major enemies of all prophets, prophetic people, and prophetic churches, hubs, and ministries. You cannot and must not leave Jezebel unchecked! There are wise strategies and sure methods for dealing with this destructive demon, but it must be addressed.

The Jezebel spirit is a spiritual assassin that takes particular aim at all things prophetic. To more fully understand this, let's dive deeper into one of the key components of prophetic ministry and one of the Bible's most legendary assassinations orchestrated by the Jezebel spirit.

> As they departed, Jesus began to say to the crowds concerning John, "What did you go out into the wilderness to see? A reed shaken by the wind? If not, what did you go out to see? A man dressed in soft clothing? Indeed, those who wear soft clothing are in kings' houses. Then what did you go out to see? A prophet? Yes, I say to you, and more than a prophet. For this is he of whom it is written:
>
> 'Look, I am sending My messenger before Your face, who will prepare Your way before You.'
>
> Truly I say to you, among those who are born of women, there has risen no one greater than John the Baptist. But he who is least in the kingdom of heaven is greater than he."
>
> —MATTHEW 11:7–11

John the Baptist was known for his preaching of repentance and his declaration of Jesus as the Messiah. It is interesting that Jesus asks the people in this passage, "What did you go…to see? A reed shaken by the wind?" This could mean a variety of things, but I want to take a prophetic spin on this. I believe that John was shaken by the winds of the Spirit, shaken by prophetic utterance, shaken by a realm of *nabi* (bubble up) preaching. Words and messages burst forth from his belly with authority and power.

John was untamed. He occupied the wilderness places. He was not a polished prophet. He did not give a variety of prophetic predictions as other Old Testament prophets did. He released a relatively simple message, yet it catapulted him to the front of the line in Jesus's assessment of Old Testament prophets. He topped the list!

John was a messenger. All prophets are some type of messenger. The means of communication and the style of release differ greatly based on the particular mantle, but they are messengers. There are various realms of the prophetic, different functions and diverse flows, but every prophetic revelation contains a message that at the end of the day points back to Jesus.

Prophets were and are those who prepare the ground for the seed. They speak what we have not yet seen, revealing that which can be seen in the realm of the spirit. They are by nature forerunners. This is critical in our understanding of why Jezebel hates the prophetic anointing. This evil spirit despises the work of true prophetic ministry because it prepares generations, regions, peoples, and nations for the move of God. It prepares the way. John prepared the way for Jesus, and this is what I believe Jesus was commending. Jesus referenced John as the greatest because he was chosen in the gap between covenants to prepare for the greatest spiritual transition since the fall of Adam. He was chosen to be the messenger to make the decree of all decrees. He was the forerunner to usher in the Christ.

What is a forerunner? It is someone who goes out ahead. Anything and everything prophetic has a forerunner nature. Prophets, prophecy, and prophetic flow always reveal what is in the heart and mind of God. As God's heart and mind come into the space that we occupy, they burst forth carrying divine power. The release of a forerunner word is the momentum in the spirit to carry a person into the manifestation of what has been spoken. The revelation carries the power of manifestation. A prophetic word is not an abstract promise but a spiritual reality. When God speaks prophetically, you are carried beyond the human and natural dimension into the limitless realm of the spirit, where all things are possible. Prophetic forerunners move out ahead in order to make a way for those that will come. They blaze spiritual trails. They open up revelations.

SEDUCTION IS HER GAME

For Herod had laid hold of John, bound him, and put him in prison for the sake of Herodias, his brother Philip's wife. For John said to him, "It is not lawful for you to have her." When Herod would have put him to death, he feared the crowd, because they counted him as a prophet.

But when Herod's birthday was celebrated, the daughter of Herodias danced before them and pleased Herod. Therefore he promised with an oath to give her whatever she would ask. Being previously instructed by her mother, she said, "Give me John the Baptist's head on a platter." The king was sorry. Nevertheless, for the oath's sake and those who sat with him at supper, he commanded it to be given to her. He sent and beheaded John in the prison. His head was brought on a platter and given to the girl, and she brought it to her mother. His disciples came and took up the body and buried it. And they went and told Jesus.

—MATTHEW 14:3–12

John the Baptist was murdered at the request of a demon-possessed woman. This was not natural anger but spiritual rage. John refused to endorse the unlawful union of the king and his new love. This is one of the attributes of rugged prophets—they will not bow to spiritual pressure when they perceive that something is wrong. They cannot be bought, intimidated, or manipulated. When they have heard the clear voice of the Lord, they become resolute. John was unwavering in his condemnation of this relationship.

The Jezebel spirit is an immoral demon. It uses various means to seduce its victims. One of its manifestations is sexual seduction. In this story we see a twofold perversion. First, Herodias captured the attention of the king so he would come into immoral relationship with her. Second, she used the allure of her daughter's dance to capture the attention of Herod and several men to ask for the head of the leading prophet.

Seduction was used to order the assassination of a mighty forerunner. These same powers are at work today, attempting to annihilate the destinies, ministries, and spiritual exploits of prophetic leaders. Jezebel has strategic plans of distraction and deception. The Jezebel spirit had John's head cut off! There is so much revelation in this assassination. This spirit understands that if it successfully attacks the head, then it can kill the body. Many times men and women, chosen by God, begin to lead a charge toward change and reformation, but the Jezebel spirit bombards them with a multipronged attack in order to cut off the head of destiny!

Jezebel loves to intimidate prophets and prophetic people. This spirit wants to send prophets into hiding. It accomplishes this in a variety of ways. As Jezebel was empowered by a weak and wicked leader named Ahab, the true prophets suffered greatly.

> When Jezebel killed the prophets of the LORD, Obadiah took a hundred prophets and hid them in groups of fifty in a cave and fed them with bread and water.
>
> —1 KINGS 18:4

The prophets were forced into the cave. Jezebel was on a murderous rampage, determined to slaughter the voice of the Lord in the land. God's prophets had to go into hiding. They could not minister. They could not flow. They could not give revelation to the people or the land because they were hiding in the cave.

The Jezebel spirit comes to push the prophetic anointing into the cave. It comes to tear down prophetic ministries and overwhelm prophetic leaders. It comes to steal the joy, rob the life, zap the strength, and quench the power. The prophets were struggling and had little provision. They survived but did not thrive. Jezebel will try to cut off the finances of prophetic ministry and prophetic people. Jezebel does not want you sowing into the prophetic voice of the Lord in the earth. It wants the prophets dead or hidden and struggling.

There is another dimension of the cave that we must think about with extreme honesty. Prophets can be peculiar people depending on their call and makeup. The way they function, the way they process, or their bold personalities can cause people to misunderstand them. As with any forerunner call, there is also a level of frontline warfare that emerges.

Jezebel may not be able to put you in a literal cave, but it will try to get you to live in a cave of rejection. Many prophets wear rejection as a badge. Instead of becoming intimate glory carriers, they manifest wounds and bitterness. Jesus came to set you and me free from the cave. We must determine not to put ourselves in a cave of rejection, a cave of isolation, or a cave of fear.

When the Jezebel spirit runs rampant, it pushes prophets into the cave. This spirit sends waves of depression over prophets so that they end up alone, contemplating their demise. It releases words of witchcraft and spirits of fear to send the prophets and prophetic people running for their lives.

> But I have a few things against you: You permit that woman Jezebel, who calls herself a prophetess, to teach and seduce My servants to commit sexual immorality and eat food sacrificed to idols.
>
> —REVELATION 2:20

Hundreds of years after the actual human being named Jezebel died, Jesus gave this strong indictment of the church in Thyatira because of their allowance of Jezebel's illegal prophetic activities. He was railing against the acceptance of witchcraft in place of authentic prophetic ministry. This realm of the Jezebel spirit is particularly toxic.

A Jezebel spirit does its best to establish its own renegade prophetic ministry through seduction. It seduces leaders with gifts, flattery, finances, and false loyalty. Jezebel proves its spirituality with grandiose proclamations of fasting, prayer, and revelation. The Jezebel spirit is a deeply rebellious spirit that will not submit to ordained leadership in any way, shape, or form.

A person operating in a Jezebel spirit can "fake it" for a time in order to be handed the reins of authority. It is a dangerous game of deception and seduction in an attempt to wrestle power away from God-ordained leaders, only to fulfill its own wicked agenda. This is the overthrow nature of Jezebel—to take the reins of power from those whom God has appointed. This spirit will move through people pledging loyalty and alliance, but it is deceptive.

STRANGE FIRE BURNS

One of the tactics that the Jezebel spirit employs is false prophetic witchcraft. Jezebel is a bewitching spirit. To more fully understand this, we must explore the nature of witchcraft.

> For rebellion is as the sin of witchcraft, and stubbornness is as iniquity and idolatry. Because you have rejected the word of the LORD, He has also rejected you from being king.
>
> —1 SAMUEL 15:23

The first component of witchcraft is rebellion. This was the Lord's harsh indictment against Saul as he openly disobeyed the instructions of heaven. He refused to do what God said. The Lord exposes a root desire of witchcraft in rebellion. The dictionary offers a simple definition of the word *rebellion*: "opposition to one in authority or dominance."[1]

It is no mistake that God's government is established as a theocracy. It is not a democracy with voting, individual rights, opinions, and preferences. In fact, when we become disciples of Jesus, we are invited into a lifestyle of surrender. The apostle Paul, who we know was a powerful early church apostle, referred to himself as a bondservant (Rom. 1:1, NKJV). A bondservant was one who had been set free legally but chose to stay in the house. To commemorate this decision, the bondservant's ear would be pierced straight through at the doorpost of the house. (See Exodus 21:5–6 and Deuteronomy 15:16–17.) This is a powerful prophetic picture. One who was freed decided to remain. I believe Paul more deeply demonstrated this surrendered lifestyle when he wrote, "'All things are lawful for me,' but not all things are helpful" (1 Cor. 10:23). He was teaching the church. He was stating that he did not live a life of navigating the narrow road because of law and legalism but because of grace. Through Jesus he was set free from the law, but he chose to remain attached to the ways of the Lord. He said no to some things because they were not wise for him as an apostle.

The bondservant has his ear pressed to the doorpost of the house. He is listening to the heartbeat of the house. This is another prophetic picture. God wants to bring us so in tune with His voice and His desires that we hear the secret whispers of His heart and know His ways. This type of intimacy fuels a life of power and exploits.

A bondservant surrenders. Witchcraft refuses surrender. A bondservant submits to authority. Witchcraft lusts for quick power and dominance. A bondservant is disciplined. A witch is unbridled. A bondservant is humble. A witch is arrogant and boastful. A bondservant lives to please the master. A witch lives to serve and please self.

Witchcraft is self-focused, self-promoting, self-serving, and self-pleasing. Jezebel is a witch.

The book of Leviticus tells of Nadab and Abihu, who were sons of Aaron and therefore priests.

> Now Nadab and Abihu, the sons of Aaron, each took his censer and put fire in it, and put incense on it, and offered strange fire before the LORD, which He did not command them to do. Then a fire came out from the LORD and devoured them, and they died before the LORD. Then Moses said to Aaron, "This is what the LORD spoke, saying: 'I will be sanctified by those who come near Me; and before all the people I will be glorified.'" And Aaron held his peace.
> —LEVITICUS 10:1–3

The priests were struck dead for playing with strange fire. This is a picture of the power of witchcraft being judged by God. Witchcraft operates in the realm of strange fire. Witchcraft taps into spiritual dimensions that are not holy. Priests are called to be holy—separated and set apart.

I have had several alarming examples of the Jezebel spirit and strange fire. Not long ago I traveled to another nation to preach. While standing on the platform, I was suddenly swept up into the realm of heavenly vision. I saw witchcraft intermingling with the prophetic. I saw prophets being seduced by the spirit of witchcraft. I began to say what I saw and to intercede for that nation.

After the meeting, I was eating in the back room with a prophet who shared startling confirmation of what I had seen. He told me about a group of prophets who had sold themselves to the powers of the enemy for fame, money, and power. They were preaching in large meetings, with masses of people coming to see them. They had detailed information from the realm of the spirit, but they had obtained it through illegal access.

This is an imperative prophetic truth! The motive behind a word is as critical in discerning it as the content of the word itself. You must listen with wisdom when prophetic things are declared. Jezebel spirits will use flattering words to gain access to people. If a person gives himself over strongly enough to false fire, he can tap into information. He receives communication from the spirit realm and knows things, but it is the communication of devils and cannot produce life or reveal the heart of God. If you listen to the word and discern the motive, you can identify that it is strange fire.

I had a very interesting encounter with a witch some time ago. The woman started coming to our church, telling people she was very prophetic. She tried her best to gain access to me.

She was very nice, but I had a subtle check. It was not a big check, just something down deep on the inside that did not feel right. She began to pursue a member of my family. She did nice things, volunteered, helped, and gave gifts. She shared little words of encouragement that were accurate and got the attention of my family member.

I was riding in the car with my wife one day, and we were having a conversation about our future and possible ministry assignments. We were talking details, places, times, etc. Within moments this person messaged someone in my family and attempted to prophesy about our conversation. She knew some of the things we had discussed. That could easily have been a prophetic operation if the mind and the character of the Lord were in it, but in this case they weren't. I believe demons relayed the information.

As time unfolded, the Lord made it very clear to me that we were dealing with a witch who was trying to infiltrate our prophetic circle. One night I lay in bed deeply grieved. The Lord began to speak to me about the person and her past. He told me what to look up and even gave me instructions to research the person's background online. In twenty-four hours, based on the word of the Lord, massive corruption was uncovered. The Lord divinely enlightened me and protected me from lying powers of witchcraft.

This is why discerning the spirits is so important. Strange fire has spiritual power, manifestation, and even information, but it is not holy. The heart of God is not in it. The character of God is not in it. Anytime someone appears very powerful in the realm of the spirit but is dishonest, is greedy, has poor family relationships, or has a bad track record, you must be cautious. I fear that often strange fire manifests, deceiving God's people to unloose evil plans against them.

I do not write this to put fear in you but to arm you for battle and effectively equip you. There is no time to be distracted or delayed. Strange fire works through Jezebel, releasing false prophetic utterances and unholy encounters. We must rightly identify and avoid these spirits and their agendas.

Years ago I was asked to be part of a business opportunity. It sounded like a dream come true. One of the people involved was highly skilled in this arena. There was just one problem: something deep inside me was unsettled. After wrestling with this but not having any confirmation on my hesitancy, I decided to override my concerns and go forward. I determined that my reservations were just my mind wavering. I announced my decision, and we were going forward.

That same night I was lying in bed and could not sleep. At about 12:30 a.m. my phone went off. A dear friend messaged me with an urgent request to speak to me. I knew that I needed to hear what my friend had to say. I felt compelled to get on the phone right then. When God speaks, you must obey, no matter how foolish or extreme it seems.

I called my friend, who began to warn me about doing business with this person. Not only was there a horrible track record of deception, but there was also a history of manipulation and Jezebelian activity. Now all my concerns were validated, and I knew that I had heard from God. That night I reversed course and canceled the agreement. A warning saved me years of possible trouble.

How can you properly discern the Jezebel spirit, strange fire, witchcraft, or false prophetic ministry? There are a few pieces of advice I would give. Number one: examine the motive. Proverbs 4:23 warns us to guard our hearts. We are to purify our hearts, examine our motives, and allow Holy Spirit to search us and reveal any improper agenda.

The Jezebel spirit always has an agenda. There is a wrong motive behind every activity of Jezebel. One of the ways you can properly discern the Jezebel spirit is by examining motive. Another way is by examining fruit. Most of the encounters I have had with this spirit have been with people who have had a track record of sowing discord, dishonor, and bad character. We should look at the fruit in the life of a person who wants to speak into our lives.

Also examine the methodology. We will explore this deeper in the book. A Jezebel spirit does things in a sneaky way to avoid proper oversight because it is a rebellious spirit. A Jezebel spirit is a forceful rank breaker that regards no one but itself. It will dishonor leaders and breach protocol every time. Whenever these behaviors are rampant, there is a wrong spirit.

POINTS TO CONSIDER

» Have you encountered someone with bad character or a bad track record trying to dominate you with prophetic words, leadings, etc., and had a concern? Don't override the check! It may save your life.

» Jezebel goes after the prophetic. It tries to cut off the head. Pray over your own life. Pray over the lives of those you know who carry a prophetic anointing.

» Are you keeping yourself in a surrendered lifestyle as a bondservant? This is a freedom key.

WHERE TO BEGIN

» Learn to examine motives. Recognize that the *why* is as important as the *what*.

» Be a person of integrity. Value character, not just gifting.

» Beware of people who have no stability but always want to give a word to others.

» Ministry flows from covenant and relationship. Ask the Lord for a covenant heart.

PRAYER

I thank You, Lord, that I am not deceived. I hear Your voice and obey Your leading. I ask for clear discernment of any and all wrong relationships and motives coming into my life. I want to love and value Your bride. I want to be a person of mercy and grace. I do not want to accuse, attack, and criticize everyone, but I do want to walk in wisdom. Help me walk in wisdom and clear discernment. In Jesus's name, amen.

Chapter 4

JEZEBEL'S SEDUCTION, SCHEMES, AND STRATEGIES

EVERYTHING THAT SATAN does is a counterfeit. He cannot create anything and is powerless over the Most High God. In order to buffet the life of a believer who is hidden in Christ, he looks for an entry point. He and his minions continually study the lives of human beings, paying close attention to their words, actions, pain, and temptation. Demonic powers utilize human weakness to create entry points for domination and strongholds. It is the ambition of the kingdom of darkness to overthrow the plans of the kingdom of God. Nothing brings greater pleasure to the hounds of hell than tormenting God's people and interrupting heavenly plans.

COUNTERFEIT REALITIES

One of the most evident examples of an attempt by evil powers to interrupt kingdom plans is the spiritual battle the apostle Paul faced. Paul was converted through a dramatic encounter with Jesus on the Damascus Road. He was launched into a series of supernatural experiences with the Lord that sent him forth into the calling on his life. This was not a simple conversion and release of a student into the ministry. This was a man supernaturally changed and carrying a mantle to help father the early church. His ministry was turning the known world upside down as the spirit of revival spread from place to place with bold preaching, in-depth teaching, radical miracles, signs, wonders, salvations, and Holy Ghost baptisms.

The mantle that Paul was carrying quickly became a target for the artillery of hell. Paul was spending countless hours praying in the spirit and receiving heavy revelation from God.

Paul decreed in 1 Corinthians 14:18, "I thank my God that I speak in tongues more than you all." As he spent time in prayer unraveling the mysteries of God, he was given foundational truths to be used as building blocks for the early church.

> But I reveal to you, brothers, that the gospel which was preached by me is not according to man. For I neither received it from man, neither was I taught it, except by a revelation of Jesus Christ.
> —GALATIANS 1:11–12

Paul was carrying uncommon revelation and authority. His teaching was fueling the move of God because the truths were being captured directly from the heart and mind of God. This type of powerful ministry posed a significant threat to the plans of darkness. The enemy could not allow Paul's ministry to go unchallenged, so hell mobilized a counterattack.

> And lest I should be exalted above measure by the abundance of revelations, a thorn was given me in the flesh, a messenger of Satan, to torment me, lest I be exalted above measure.
> —2 CORINTHIANS 12:7

There was a demonic entity assigned to the life of Paul to harass him and shut him down. There was a demon stalking him, creating havoc, struggle, and turmoil. This provides stunning clarity about spiritual warfare strategies. Let's examine a few foundational truths in order to more clearly comprehend satanic tactics.

Things in the realm of the spirit are governed by laws. There is divine order in the kingdom of God. Nothing is done randomly or without authorization. God always has a clear-cut chain of command. He reveals this to us over and over in Scripture.

> Then God said, "Let us make man in our image, after our likeness, and let them have dominion over the fish of the sea, and over the birds of the air, and over the livestock, and over all the earth, and over every creeping thing that creeps on the earth." So God created man in His own image; in the image of God He created him; male and female He created them.
>
> —Genesis 1:26–27

When God created mankind, He placed the inhabitants of the earth under the authority of His creation. Man had all power and dominion. The enemy had absolutely no authority whatsoever; that is why he had to persuade man to cooperate with his plans to breach authority and gain influence over mankind. Satan could do nothing without the willing cooperation of Adam and Eve. When they yielded to sin and disobeyed God, it changed the order in the earth.

> And to Adam He said, "Because you have listened to the voice of your wife and have eaten from the tree about which I commanded you, saying, 'You shall not eat of it,' cursed is the ground on account of you; in hard labor you will eat of it all the days of your life. Thorns and thistles it will bring forth for you, and you will eat the plants

71

of the field. By the sweat of your face you will eat bread until you return to the ground, because out of it you were taken; for you are dust, and to dust you will return."

—GENESIS 3:17–19

Man was put under a curse because of the unlawful activities of Adam and Eve. It would take a redemptive plan to restore the authority.

So it is written, "The first man Adam was made a living soul." The last Adam was made a life-giving spirit.

—1 CORINTHIANS 15:45

KINGDOM GOVERNMENT

Jesus is called the second Adam. He was birthed to redeem, or to buy back, mankind and undo the curse of sin. He was of divine origin, as was the first Adam, yet a man living in a fleshly body and enduring temptation. He was the sacrifice for sin and the Lamb that was slain. He came to break the power of hell and reverse the curse.

Christ has redeemed us from the curse of the law by being made a curse for us—as it is written, "Cursed is everyone who hangs on a tree"—so that the blessing of Abraham might come on the Gentiles through Jesus Christ, that we might receive the promise of the Spirit through faith.

—GALATIANS 3:13–14

In every area there is an authority structure. In our homes there is a godly order and chain of command.

Wives, be submissive to your own husbands as unto the Lord. For the husband is the head of the wife, just as

Christ is the head and Savior of the church, which is His body. But as the church submits to Christ, so also let the wives be to their own husbands in everything. Husbands, love your wives, just as Christ also loved the church and gave Himself for it.

—EPHESIANS 5:22–25

Husbands are commanded to love and cherish their wives. They are instructed to arise as spiritual leaders, providing prayer, protection, and godly direction in union with their wives. Children are admonished to obey the instructions of their parents.

Children, obey your parents in the Lord, for this is right. "Honor your father and mother," which is the first commandment with a promise, "so that it may be well with you and you may live long on the earth."

—EPHESIANS 6:1–3

We are encouraged to pray for those in authority over us.

Therefore I exhort first of all that you make supplications, prayers, intercessions, and thanksgivings for everyone, for kings and for all who are in authority, that we may lead a quiet and peaceful life in all godliness and honesty.

—1 TIMOTHY 2:1–2

In the government of the kingdom of God there are established roles, responsibilities, and ranks. There is not a random placement of people but a strategic development of gifts, callings, and offices to lead and guide God's people. This point is further illustrated with the language used in this scripture:

> And God hath set some in the church, first apostles, secondarily prophets, thirdly teachers, after that miracles, then gifts of healings, helps, governments, diversities of tongues.
>
> —1 Corinthians 12:28, kjv

The word *set* here means fixed, placed, or established.[1] The Lord Himself places men and women in roles of divine leadership. When He establishes them in those roles, there is a measure of authority granted to fulfill the responsibility. There is also an anointing or divine enablement released upon their lives. Prophets are anointed to prophesy. Teachers are anointed to teach; it flows out of them with ease because they have been given a spiritual portion. With these ranks and responsibilities there comes a demand for character. All too often we witness the tragic fall of highly gifted men and women who had tremendous power but very poor fruit.

At the forefront of the government of God are two offices: the apostle and the prophet. This does not in any way mean that they are more valuable or important than any other office or gift. It simply means that they bear a greater responsibility and have a higher level of governing authority. To illustrate this point, the Bible says God set the apostle first (1 Cor. 12:28). The word *first* here is the Greek word *prōton*, meaning "firstly (in time, place, order, or importance):—before, at the beginning, chiefly (at, at the) first (of all)."[2] It is quite clear that the Bible is establishing rank. Apostles are like generals tasked with receiving and releasing revelation that pushes the body forward. They are given plans for regions, peoples, and nations. They are called to teach and clear up confusion in key areas. They are God's generals. Beside them are the prophets, great and dynamic spiritual forerunners who go out ahead in revelation, clearing the path for the people of God.

God works on the earth through His ekklesia, His ruling and governing people. He has a rank, authority, and structure. He releases divine revelation, powerful anointing, and angelic assistance to get the job done—on earth as it is in heaven! This is the goal: to release the kingdom of God on earth, to release the authority of the risen Christ on earth, subduing and overwhelming the powers of hell. The Lord is mantling people who will fight against and overcome the powers of hell.

Satan has a counterfeit government. He delegates various powers and strategies to his dark army.

> For we wrestle not against flesh and blood, but against principalities, against powers, against the rulers of the darkness of this world, against spiritual wickedness in high places.
>
> —EPHESIANS 6:12, KJV

- **Principalities** are the highest-ranking ruling spirits assigned to territories, regions, nations, and people groups. The Greek word indicates the primary or highest authority.[3] These demonic forces are given charge to bind and hold territories. We see a picture of this in the Old Testament in Daniel 10 concerning the prince of Persia, who is a ruling spirit. Principalities will come in direct conflict with apostles and apostolic ministry because they are also assigned to regions and peoples.

- **Powers** are the second-highest-ranking spirits that carry a manifestation of supernatural power to enforce the plans of the principalities. They influence the thoughts and feelings of human beings, seeding the thought realm with demonic lies. They work hard to destroy kingdom order, rule, and reign. The meaning of the word *powers* indicates supernatural force and manifestation.[4] These spirits operate in heavy divination, false fire, counterfeit spiritual manifestation, and evil supernatural operations. Powers attempt to overthrow prophets and prophetic ministry.

- **Rulers of darkness** release deception, false religion, and the occult. They work to bind the souls of men and women in foul deception. These demons sow the seeds of false belief systems, directly combatting the office of the teacher.

- **Spiritual wickedness** releases lust for sin and depravity. Spiritual wickedness dwells in the high places, the airspace above the earth. Both angels and demons travel through a great highway known as the first and second heavens. If our spiritual eyes were opened, we would see the spiritual activity taking place in the heavens and all around us. These demonic beings mirror the evangelist, serving as the recruiting arm of the kingdom of darkness. These spirits use supernatural enticement to draw people in to dark plans and schemes. They draw people to darkness much as the evangelist draws people to the kingdom of God.

- **Demons** are the foot soldiers in the kingdom of darkness, carrying out the plans of the ruling spirits. They are sent on assignment and vary in category depending on their particular purpose. Demons are continually on the move, implementing the plans of darkness and attempting to create bondage in the lives of human beings. Just as a pastor tends to the needs of individual people, so these demons tend to evil assignments against the lives of people.

DEMONIC PARTNERSHIPS

The Jezebel spirit is a ruling spirit that partners with evil powers to manifest manipulation and witchcraft. One of the powers the Jezebel spirit employs is seduction. Wherever the Jezebel spirit is at work, there is seduction at hand. The word *seduce* means "to persuade to disobedience or disloyalty; to lead astray usually by persuasion or false promises; to carry out the physical seduction of."[5] The Jezebel spirit comes with enticement to lure people away from ordained plans, purposes, and order. There are layers in the seduction strategy of Jezebel.

In her book *Jezebel's Puppets*, Jennifer LeClaire wrote a plot summary for Jezebel: "A wicked spirit that has roamed the earth for thousands of years seeking someone to entice into sin, Jezebel is more than the spirit of control and manipulation that many make it out to be. Jezebel is a spirit of seduction that works to woo people into immorality and idolatry—but it doesn't work alone. With the help of Ahab, false prophets, and faithful servants, Jezebel has been sinking its seductive teeth into society for ages—and has infiltrated the pulpit and the pews of the church. Since few see Jezebel for what it is, this spirit continues to secure the hearts and minds of those who claim Jesus as their first and true love. Will Jezebel ultimately lead the church into a great falling away, or will the church wake up to this perversion before it's too late?"[6]

One of the ways that Jezebel seduces people is by speaking to their ambitions. When a Jezebel spirit comes into a ministry, it will often work to entangle key leaders and people by speaking to their ambitions. It will prophesy to a key leader that he should really be the senior leader. It will speak to the wounds in the heart of a person and validate pain in order to gain access. It can also reveal certain hidden desires that seem to have been forgotten. It will speak accurately to those desires but from an unholy place to draw people away from their current assignments and entangle them in an evil agenda.

The spirit of Jezebel is a sexually impure spirit. The spirit of whoredom is one of Jezebel's defiled cohorts. The whoredom of Jezebel includes prostitution, fornication, adultery, and all manner of evil sexual sins. Much of the rampant sexual sin that we see in the world and in the church today is rooted in the seduction of Jezebel.

> And it came to pass, when Joram saw Jehu, that he said, Is it peace, Jehu? And he answered, What peace, so long as the whoredoms of thy mother Jezebel and her witchcrafts are so many?
>
> —2 KINGS 9:22, KJV

Jezebel partnered with the prince of the power of the air to release constant bombardment of filthy entertainment devised to lower inhibitions and seduce people. At the heart of witchcraft and idol worship are impure sexual practices. The very act of sex itself creates a deep and lasting bond in the participants' hearts, and even an emotional or mental affair can cause irreparable damage to a marriage.

> You have heard that it was said by the ancients, "You shall not commit adultery." But I say to you that whoever

looks on a woman to lust after her has committed adultery with her already in his heart.

—MATTHEW 5:27–28

There is an emotional, soulish seduction that precedes a physical act. The seduction of Jezebel will always begin in the mind. In the arts and entertainment industry Jezebel has systematically lowered the resistance to sex and perversion for generations until almost anything goes now. As the web of seduction has been cast over minds, confusion and bondage have unfolded with devastating effects. I have personally prayed with countless young people who have been gravely addicted to pornography with easy access on their smartphones. It has been a progressive and evil plan intended to chip away biblical values and covenant relationships.

This whoredom spirit is not only a sexual issue but a covenant issue. Where you find the spirit of whoredom there is a breaking of vows, a lack of faithfulness, and self-serving behavior. Whoredom sells itself, its gift, its talent, for gain. It will quickly break a relationship for another opportunity. This spirit linked with Jezebel has defiled ministry relationships and aborted the concept of family in the kingdom.

THE PIT

Jezebel creates a deep and dark pit of sorrow as it seduces its victims and brings them into a place of defilement. In ministry this spirit lacks any kind of faithfulness and will cause people to jump from place to place with no root system. As they yield to this spirit, they will eventually wind up trapped in its pit.

79

> For a whore is a deep ditch; and a strange woman is a
> narrow pit. She also lieth in wait as for a prey, and
> increaseth the transgressors among men.
>
> —PROVERBS 23:27–28, KJV

Over the years, I have often seen a spirit of Jezebel come into a ministry that I was leading or the ministry of one of my friends with an agenda to disrupt and cause problems. I have prayed through and worked through deep and troubling challenges brought on by people with this spirit. When Jezebel comes into a church or ministry, it is sneaky and subtle, yet intensely wicked. Jezebel thrives where there is an Ahab type of leader who will overlook its cunning manipulation. People with Jezebel spirits are often highly gifted individuals who offer goods, services, finances, or assistance, but there is always a price to pay.

Some years ago I took a small team with me to a powerful church where I was going to be preaching. I will never forget the encounter we had with a boisterous individual who attended that church. This person seemed unstable, had been married several times, and kept stalking the ministers. At the time, this person was focused on an determined to marry a powerful minister. That type of behavior in and of itself freaks me out!

I was at this church for a series of meetings, and the person of whom I am speaking kept finding a way into the back room, into conversations, into events. This individual's presence became increasingly uncomfortable. Finally one of my team members pulled me aside to ask me if I had observed these behaviors. Of course I said yes, and we both agreed that it was a spirit of Jezebel. This individual kept trying to gain access to me, offering gifts, money, etc., but I discerned the motive and wanted no part of it.

Finally my team and I asked the leaders of the church if they had discerned the spirit. To our amazement, they said yes but indicated they were afraid to deal with it. You could have knocked me over with a feather, I was so shocked! They knew that there was a Jezebel spirit slithering and maneuvering in their midst, yet they had determined to allow it? Why? The answer is simple. They recognized the severity of the manifestation if they confronted it.

I have seen entire ministries destroyed by retaliation from a Jezebel spirit. It is imperative that you not allow that to bring fear but simply arm yourself with the wisdom of God. If you pick a fight with a demon, you need to be ready. It is not something that you just casually do. It takes authority, strategy, and wisdom to win the war.

THREE PHASES OF THE JEZEBEL SPIRIT

I believe that every spirit of Jezebel that enters a ministry will go through three phases. I have developed this teaching through the years to help equip church and ministry leaders when discerning and confronting this manipulative spirit.

1. Entry
Jezebel looks for vulnerable people to influence and disciple. In a church it will search out the weak, the hurting, those who can be manipulated through prophetic words. In a family or relational setting it will arrive looking to gain avenues of influence.

In ministries Jezebel will begin a network of gossip with secret "prayer" calls and conversations, laying the groundwork for a future rebellion. It keeps these contacts hidden beneath the cover of darkness to avoid exposure.

It attempts to infiltrate any and all prayer and prophetic

ministries. It will attempt to join the intercession team and become a part of the prophetic team.

It uses flattery. In a ministry it will flatter the leader with big compliments and grandiose spiritual pronouncements. In family and relationships it will offer self-serving commitments to gain favor with the intended target(s).

It will babysit the leader's kids, wash the cars, run errands, and give gifts. A Jezebel spirit will release funds, offer money, and lavish gifts on a person, people, or leaders, all in an attempt to gain influence. This spirit lusts for power!

It boasts of revelation. It will reveal how spiritual it is—how much the person fasts, prays, and seeks God. It will exalt itself in the realm of spirituality far above others. This is a conquer strategy.

It searches for a position and always has a hidden agenda.

2. Exposure

This is the messy phase of the Jezebel ordeal. In a church or ministry, this phase is critical.

After many hidden schemes, the behaviors of a Jezebel spirit begin to unravel, and those involved start to see the problem at hand. Once this spirit recognizes it is at risk of being exposed, it will work overtime to rally allies. In a church or ministry it will try to build a coalition of people to stand with it. In a family struggle it will pit one member against the other.

It will boldly state that the ministry or church leaders are not spiritual enough and do not accurately hear from God. It will say that God is not pleased with the ministry and make wicked pronouncements over a place.

This spirit then exerts strong control and emotional manipulation over followers, demanding loyalty. In a family it will create a split, and in a ministry it will quickly build a coalition of offended, weak people to stand with it. It will prophesy to their wounds and gain their loyalty.

When the demand for submission comes from a leader, Jezebel will boldly and unashamedly refuse to submit. This spirit is a foul, rank-breaking demon that recognizes no authority and exists to tear down godly structure and rank.

3. Confrontation

When the confrontation happens, the person with the Jezebel spirit will voice opposition and stand firm in a position of independence. The Jezebel spirit will not bow to any type of leader.

People with the Jezebel spirit will boldly declare that God is on their side. This is all part of the deception. Even though people with the Jezebel spirit are acting in direct contradiction to the Word of God, Jezebel will not bend. It does not recognize the authority of the Word of God and will twist Scripture to justify its case.

This spirit will display huge emotional outbursts and tantrums to disrupt and distract. Every time I have ever encountered a Jezebel spirit in operation, I have witnessed a strong measure of emotional manipulation. This will manifest through tears, anger, sorrow, and blame shifting. The Jezebel spirit will attempt to place guilt on the one who is righteous and get the attention off itself.

The end result is an intense power struggle. In a church or ministry there must be a choice: either the people will follow the senior leader or they will not. Jezebel and the leader cannot peacefully coexist, as it is the mission of this spirit to destroy the leader. This is the harsh reality. There will be a showdown, and the people must make a choice. This is where strong prophetic ministry is vital. The prophets can expose what is happening and empower the people to see it from a spiritual rather than an emotional standpoint.

In a family or relationship the process is much the same. Choices have to be made. Will people allow and tolerate the maneuvering of Jezebel? Lines must be drawn. Humble repentance needs to take place to bring deliverance and freedom.

When a person with a Jezebel spirit is forced out of a church or ministry, he or she will let loose the powers of witchcraft on the way out. The Jezebel spirit will release a multitude of curses, creating confusion and a demonic swirl that must be broken with strong prayer and authority. This spirit will often attempt to reach back into a church and snatch people out with manipulation and accusation.

Those who are not strong in the spirit can easily get sucked in to Jezebel's witchcraft with misplaced sympathy. They can easily watch the tantrums and feel that there has been a lack of compassion. Compassion is one of the most powerful forces in the world, but it must be properly placed. Demons will latch on to compassion and use it as a means to stay. Jezebel wants to take over! It does not just want a piece; it wants the entire cake. This is the harsh reality, but it must be recognized.

POINTS TO CONSIDER

» Have you experienced emotional manipulation from the Jezebel spirit?

» Do you know someone who exhibits these characteristics?

» Launching out in a confrontation without prayer and wisdom can lead to utter chaos!

» The place to begin is prayer. Ask the Lord for insight, strength, and wisdom.

» Demons only respond to firm faith and authority.

» As a leader, have you been confronted by the operation of a Jezebel spirit on some level? Have you experienced its seduction drawing you away from kingdom purposes?

» You must never allow this spirit to continue to maneuver in your midst.

WHERE TO BEGIN

» First review some of the symptoms listed in this chapter.

» Ask Holy Spirit to shine His light on your own heart. Proper self-examination is key.

» Pray for greater discerning of spirits and wisdom in relationships.

» Recognize the reality of the spirit realm and its impact on your life.

PRAYER

Father, I come before You seeking purity. I do not want my life mixed with any impure spiritual influence. Search my heart and reveal anything that is impure. I ask that You guide me in my family, in my private life, and in my kingdom calling. Make me aware of any seducing powers of Jezebel. I come against those powers in Jesus's name and forbid their operation in my life. I claim purity over my life, and I claim wisdom and discernment. In Jesus's name, amen.

Chapter 5

CASTING DOWN THE DEMON QUEEN JEZEBEL

J EZEBEL IS FOUND as a character in the Old Testament. She was used to defile God's people, tear down the altars of God, release demonic Baal worship, engage in seduction, destroy the prophetic ministry in the land, and pollute the kingdom. She was a demon-possessed witch masquerading as a prophet. She was no true prophet but one who carried strange fire and evil utterances.

CONQUEST BRINGS CONTAMINATION

Ahab the son of Omri did more evil in the sight of the LORD than all who were before him. The sins of Jeroboam the son of Nebat were seen as minor for him to walk in, for he took Jezebel the daughter of Ethbaal, king of the Sidonians, as his wife and went and served Baal and worshipped him. He raised an altar for Baal in the house of Baal, which he had built in Samaria. Ahab made an Asherah and did more to provoke the LORD God of Israel to anger than all the kings of Israel who preceded him.

—1 KINGS 16:30–33

It is impossible to fully grasp the depth of evil that took place during the reign of Ahab without proper inspection of the history of Jezebel. She was a false prophetess of the demon god Baal. She operated in powerful seduction to accomplish her will and the will of Baal. Her alignment with Ahab sent the nation into a downward spiral of wickedness and idolatry.

When Ahab came into covenant with Jezebel, he bowed to Baal. Not only did he surrender his life to false gods, but he also connected Israel to demonic idolatry. Jezebel was an instrument of the enemy used to defile God's people and corrupt the kingdom. This picture gives us insight into the plots this spirit launches today. It is a perverse spirit of domination that works to open up gateways for demonic activity to overthrow godly plans, families, ministries, and people. Jezebel is an overthrow spirit that works to overcome and subdue people for destructive purposes. An alliance with this spirit is the entry point of disaster!

Jezebel means "unmarried; un-husbanded or un-exalted; without dwelling or cohabitation."[1] This is a picture of a defiled woman who carries strong evil spirits and lacks any capacity for covenant relationship. What type of man would enter into a relationship with this woman? Jezebel was literally Jeze-baal—an ambassador and servant of the god Baal, who stood in direct opposition to Yahweh. Ahab had no business marrying this woman and forming a covenant with a covenant breaker.

The Jezebel spirit neither honors nor recognizes covenant. When this spirit operates in families, it manipulates and forms alliances to fulfill its own evil agenda. When this spirit operates in ministries, it totally disregards authority, honor, and relationship to pursue its own desires. It disguises its ambition in terminology using the name of the Lord. It is totally deceptive and demon-inspired. It is a rank-breaking devil that abhors authority and refuses any type of biblical submission. Jezebel has no regard for loyalty and typically has a long track record of bad relationships.

The Jezebel spirit cannot and will not operate without the permission of an Ahab. Jezebel will always test the strength of a leader, pushing the boundaries. In the church world those with a Jezebel spirit will hop from place to place, leaving a long wake of destruction and deception behind. It is crucial that kingdom leaders inspect fruit and know the track record of a new leader before positioning him or her in power. When you place a person with a Jezebel spirit in a position of authority, you will live to regret it; this spirit will create confusion, calamity, and demonic disruption in pursuit of its own will. Those with a Jezebel spirit may act as if they are listening, but they will not accept your instruction or correction.

HEED THE WARNINGS

Not only does the spirit of Jezebel employ seduction and sexual deviancy, but it also opens the door for spirits of infirmity and catastrophic illness.

> Look! I will throw her onto a sickbed, and those who commit adultery with her into great tribulation, unless they repent of their deeds.
> —REVELATION 2:22

At the end of a person's journey with the Jezebel spirit there is extensive sickness. I have tragically seen this happen twice in my life. The Lord will gracefully woo people over and over again to repentance. He will repeatedly send prophetic warnings, but they must heed the warnings, humble themselves, cut all affiliation with Jezebel, and truly repent, which means to completely change their thinking. Controlling personalities must dramatically change their methods of operation and thought patterns. They must undo years of learned behavior and get emotional healing along with spiritual deliverance. Cast out, reform, rethink, renew, and undo the yoke of evil spirits!

Some time ago I encountered a powerful minister who had a personality that could capture the attention of anyone. This leader could persuade you to do anything. When this person's skills were put to good use, it was like an iron in the hand of the Lord. People were forever changed. This minister took joy in pouring into people hungry for training and development in their call, and in the hands of the Lord this was a powerful gift! As I got up close, though, I also saw something else, a dark underside.

When a person did not do what this minister wanted, the minister would lash out with accusations and attacks. I had heard this person call other pastors to defame some traveling ministers because they did not do what the leader desired. The strength that I saw used in a good way was also used in a toxic capacity. As time passed, it seemed as though no one would stand up to this bullying behavior, so it went unchecked, and increased. The Jezebel spirit was running rampant with no accountability or repentance.

This minister was caught in lies on many occasions. These deceptions were tools used to manipulate the outcomes of situations to get the minister's own way. At first the lies were in private, but eventually they became bolder. Public messages were filled with deception. Stories that never happened in the person's life were made up. Struggles that were current were claimed as victories that had already been won. As Jezebel gained a stronghold, the behavior spiraled out of control. Lives were destroyed, people were broken, and hearts were wounded. This pattern of bondage would eventually create a choke hold, stifling the anointing and destroying a once-vibrant ministry. It would eventually end in ruin. Watching it from a distance was like watching a tragic play unfold, but there was little anyone could do because the Jezebel spirit had its claws deeply embedded.

This person would turn and twist facts to achieve the desired outcome. As time went by, deep paranoia and loneliness set in. Jezebel isolated the minister and created a deep well of distrust of people. Instead of love, there was bitterness. What had been a vibrant and powerful personality became weak, mean, and bitter. Occasionally you would catch a glimpse of the old flame, but it was increasingly buried deep beneath a hard exterior shell. Close personal relationships were in shambles as the Jezebel spirit grew in strength in the life of this person. God sent countless people with the mercy and compassion of the Lord to call for repentance, yet these calls went unheeded, viewed as a breach of authority. There is a lesson here: no matter who we are or what position we hold, we are all accountable on some level and need the input, oversight, and correction of godly leaders. Removing this counsel and creating a team of yes-men creates a breeding ground for the Jezebel spirit.

The story turned tragic as the minister fell prey to a series of illnesses. Eventually a final blow claimed the life of this once-powerful servant of God. This individual died filled with wounds, paranoia, and bitterness. This is the intended outcome of the evil powers of Jezebel. It wants to strip the anointing, the life, the zeal, and the purpose out of God's people. It wants to overwhelm and conquer. If allowed, Jezebel will lead a person to a bed of affliction. I am certainly not saying that all illness comes from this—there are also physical issues and attacks from the enemy. But it is a reality that Jezebel will lead a person to a sickbed.

Don't Become an Ahab

I was leading a young ministry when a man came to me to share his story of deep marital problems. This man carried such a sweet presence of the Lord. He was compassionate, sincere, and kind. He began to tell me the story of recent troubles with his wife.

This man told me that his wife had become enamored with a woman claiming to be a prophet and would not make any decision without her counsel. His wife was spending most of their money on lengthy phone conversations and then giving what was left to the woman. (This was a number of years ago, before the technology we have now, when cell phones charged for long distance and we paid by the minute.) His wife ignored his repeated warnings, refusing to submit to his instructions.

As he shared this story, my stomach began to turn, and I could feel the powers of evil attacking his family. I strongly and firmly warned him that this was not a prophet but a Jezebel spirit. I pointed out scriptures about marriage and how this spirit was ignoring the Word of God. Anything prophetic that disregards the Word is a demon spirit! I told him that he needed to stand firm, cut off the money for the phone calls, and put an end to this. I told him that I would meet with him and his wife to minister deliverance to her and break the powers of Jezebel.

He agreed with what I was saying, but there was an issue— he didn't have the strength. As I talked with him, I could see that he was indeed a man like Ahab, lacking the backbone to stand up to this demonic power. Authority is always required to break the grip of demon spirits and get them out. Jezebel is the same! You cannot be nice and passive with a Jezebel spirit. It is a vile demonic power sent to abort destinies and destroy lives. You must see it, confront it, and remove it. A leader who allows

Jezebel to stay in position is guilty of its sins. This man could not and would not operate in his authority. Instead, he allowed the situation to continue.

His wife talked him into cutting ties with our ministry because she recognized that I would not tolerate the Jezebel spirit. Years later I received devastating news. I was told the wife ended up in a sickbed and eventually died. She had drained all of their money, and their lives ended in disaster, all because of the sinister plot of Jezebel.

Ahab becomes a gateway for the operation of the Jezebel spirit. Jezebel, who married King Ahab, was the daughter of King Ethbaal of Sidon. His very name demonstrates deep-rooted idol worship. His name means "a man of Baal."[2] He was a high priest of the Canaanite fertility goddess Astarte. Many scholars agree that Astarte and the Babylonian goddess Ishtar are the same idol. Both Astarte and Ishtar were revered as fertility goddesses. They were associated with fertility, life, and sensuality.

Jezebel was raised from childhood to be a servant of demon gods. She was a loyal ally of Baal, determined to represent and worship him, along with the goddess of fertility, wherever she went, including the land of Yahweh's people. She could only do this with the submission of a wicked king who yielded to her seductive powers.

In his landmark book *Unmasking the Jezebel Spirit*, John Paul Jackson writes:

> A spirit of Ahab symbolizes the abdication of authority, or at the very least, passive authority. It bespeaks of a mind-set that avoids confrontation and denies fault. The spirit of Ahab loves the position it has and fears confrontation. Someone with an Ahab spirit would rather make

peace at any cost, even if it leads to making an unholy alliance.

An individual under the influence of an Ahab spirit often makes truces instead of covenants, thus prostituting rather than sanctifying relationships. But how can you have a truce with someone whose goal is to destroy you? It is impossible! Nonetheless, an Ahab spirit will always sacrifice the future good for the sake of peace today.

Working in tandem, the spirits of Ahab and Jezebel will quietly form a codependent relationship. Both will need and feed off the other in order to accomplish each one's goals. A pastor who is influenced by an Ahab spirit will need the help of someone influenced by a Jezebel spirit to maintain position and enlarge or entrench a powerbase.[3]

UNHOLY ALLIANCES

The kingdom of Israel was sent into a time of great trial by the unholy alliance of Ahab and Jezebel. They defiled the ways of Yahweh, exalted the altar of Baal, and permitted the unholy to take dominance. Jezebel instituted the building of stone idols atop all the high places and even in the holy Temple. She was a harlot and a witch, according to 2 Kings 9:22.

Strong, life-giving churches are built upon two dominant anointings: the apostolic and the prophetic.

> Now, therefore, you are no longer strangers and foreigners, but are fellow citizens with the saints and members of the household of God, having been built upon the foundation of the apostles and prophets, Jesus Christ Himself being the chief cornerstone.
>
> —EPHESIANS 2:19–20

As the early church was advancing with rapid success, it was the apostles who were at the forefront. The apostolic gift is a strong, bold gift! The word *apostle* means "sent one."[4] Apostles are sent to places and to people with a divine commission. They are governors who rule with supernatural wisdom, strength, and authority. They teach and train people to redeem and rebuild the mighty works of God. They activate gifts, callings, and destinies. They do not build comfortable places of rest but active centers of kingdom activity and training.

The apostolic spirit is one of strength and power. When apostles preach, they challenge the demonic powers and push back the darkness. They are not content to just leave things as they are. They are mantled to shake things up! They make demonic powers nervous. Now, there are some who falsely teach that there are no modern-day apostles. This is in error, as the book of Ephesians makes no distinction when it identifies the five ministry offices:

> He gave some to be apostles, prophets, evangelists, pastors, and teachers, for the equipping of the saints, for the work of service, and for the building up of the body of Christ.
>
> —EPHESIANS 4:11–12

The work of equipping is ongoing. It is not finished. People are being called, trained, appointed, and released today. The kingdom is growing and expanding even now. Apostles were listed first in 1 Corinthians 12:28. They were sent in as generals to lead the body into heavenly battle plans and prevail over the powers of hell. There were twelve original apostles of the Lamb who hold a unique place in the history of the church and the heavens. They are irreplaceable. Yet the office and calling of apostles continued after the original twelve and is still alive and active today, leading the mighty army of God.

The church also desperately needs prophets and prophetic ministry. It is absolutely impossible to obtain the victory without prophetic ministry. These two anointings work together to unlock kingdom plans and purposes. Prophets see in high definition. They are lifted high into heavenly places to see coming attacks, to warn, to unravel mysteries, and to be exposed to huge dreams in the heart of God for His kids. They shine bright light on the pathway for the people of God. Prophets confirm and affirm. They speak God's plans and His heart over people's lives, connecting them to eternal purposes. When prophetic ministry is functioning in a strong and healthy capacity, it creates such a life-giving flow of heaven on earth.

> Surely the Lord GOD does nothing without revealing His purpose to His servants the prophets.
>
> —AMOS 3:7

Prophets have one of the most special invitations of all— to share in the secrets of the Lord. I love to ponder Amos 3:7 because it takes me back to childhood. I can remember the game where a friend would whisper in my ear, and then I would share that same secret to another, and we'd laugh and laugh. You could not hear the secret unless you were close! Prophets and prophetic ministry require intimacy. As we live close to the Father, we are invited to explore all the vast chambers of His wonderful imagination and its immeasurable creativity. We are also invited to explore the depths of His vibrant, rich, and compassionate heart of love. Prophets ultimately reveal the heart, the mind, and the dreams of God to His people. Prophets are revealers!

These two gifts, along with the other wonderful gifts of God, powerfully equip the church to inherit the position that Jesus paid for: rulership.

> For if by one man's trespass death reigned through him, then how much more will those who receive abundance of grace and the gift of righteousness reign in life through the One, Jesus Christ.
>
> —ROMANS 5:17

Strong churches, strong ministries, and strong believers enforce the reign of Christ. They use the authority that Jesus granted and stand boldly upon the promises of God. They do not shrink back when the enemy rears his head. It takes people who know who they are in the spirit to conquer the operations of the enemy.

Apostles and apostolic ministries guard the gates. They do not allow demonic powers to keep their hold on people, places, or regions. They march forth with a strong word from God and an authority in the Spirit. The demons in the early church era knew who the apostles were because they were constantly dismantling their structures and kicking them out.

> The evil spirit answered, "I know Jesus, and I know Paul, but who are you?"
>
> —ACTS 19:15

This demon knew Paul because he was terrorizing the courts of hell. Paul was training believers to cast out demons. Paul was teaching people the truth. Paul was leading an advancing army that was arising and standing against the plans of darkness. Modern-day apostles pose a great threat to the kingdom of darkness. Regions cannot and will not be changed without spiritual warfare. There is a struggle for which kingdom will prevail, and many ministries give up before the victory comes. They need a strong apostolic anointing to push them over the top.

Don't Run and Don't Hide

Prophets are an enemy to the Jezebel spirit. One of the primary functions of the Jezebel spirit is a false prophetic ministry. During the reign of Ahab, Jezebel murdered prophets of the Lord, released tremendous intimidation, and had the remaining prophets hiding in a cave.

True prophets know how to see in the dark. They have night vision. They can discern what is going on beneath cover. They see Jezebel lurking beneath a polished exterior. When the Jezebel spirit encounters a true prophet or prophetic voice, it will unload warfare.

One of the most vivid examples of the attack of Jezebel against the prophetic is the plight of Elijah when she released a demonic word curse over him.

> And Ahab told Jezebel all that Elijah had done and how he had executed all the prophets with the sword. Then Jezebel sent a messenger to Elijah, saying, "So let the gods do to me and more also, if I do not make your life as the life of one of them by tomorrow about this time."
>
> When he saw that she was serious, he arose and ran for his life to Beersheba, which belongs to Judah, and left his servant there. But he went a day's journey into the wilderness and came and sat down under a juniper tree and asked that he might die, saying, "It is enough! Now, O Lord, take my life, for I am not better than my fathers."
>
> As he lay and slept under the juniper tree, an angel

touched him and said to him, "Arise and eat." He looked, and there was a cake baked on coals and a jar of water at his head. And he ate and drank and then lay down again.

The angel of the LORD came again a second time and touched him and said, "Arise and eat, because the journey is too great for you." He arose and ate and drank and went in the strength of that food forty days and forty nights to Horeb, the mountain of God.

—1 KINGS 19:1–8

Elijah stood atop the mountain, challenging all the false prophets of Baal, and God answered with supernatural fire. In a single act of uncommon bravery, he openly exposed the corruption of Jezebel. Her prophets were killed as a result of his victory that day. But the witch was not about to go away quietly. The prophet had prevailed over her kingdom, and she was going to counterpunch him. This is symptomatic of the Jezebel spirit; it fights the prophetic anointing tooth and nail. If exposure comes forth, it will hurl a flurry of demonic word curses and intimidating accusations. It wants to send the prophets fleeing for their very lives.

Jezebel sent a vile and corrupt message to the servant of God. She wasn't even there, but someone else carried her contaminated words upon his lips. Jezebel always works through messengers. This spirit will build demonic networks inside of ministries, teams, families, and organizations. It will seduce, lie, and intimidate to create its coalition, and then conspire with its team to overthrow true prophetic anointing.

When the utterance was released, Elijah was sent into an abnormal tailspin. He sank deep into a pit of depression. This was an absolutely shocking transformation. He went from a fearless warrior of Yahweh to a broken and intimidated man.

What could have changed so suddenly? There were a couple of factors at work.

First, he had just come from one of the most intense moments of ministry in his entire life. People often do not realize the toll that extreme times of outpouring can take on the body. When the raw and powerful anointing of God pours through people, they can feel zapped in their minds and bodies afterward. This is why protection in prayer and the right people surrounding a man or woman of God are vital. I believe Elijah was unusually susceptible to a spiritual attack because every part of his being was absolutely drained as he had warred with his mind, body, and spirit being lifted into the heavenlies and crushing the throne of darkness. Jezebel sent her message at the most opportune time for her. This spirit will come when it finds people at their most vulnerable.

Second, I believe Elijah allowed the power of Jezebel's words to overtake him by giving them consideration. The Bible says that "he saw" that she was serious. Her witchcraft opened up evil imaginations, and he did not cast them down. He could see himself being slaughtered. He could see himself being captured. He then ran for his life.

In a moment he was sent packing! This is what Jezebel wants—to plant evil seeds of corruption and defeat in the minds of prophets. This spirit works through curses in an attempt to shut down the prophetic. It is key that we stand in opposition by the authority of the name of Jesus and the power of almighty God. There is no place for fear in the heart of a warrior who has been authorized by the mighty King Jesus! Jezebel is no match for the blood of Jesus.

The Lord sent angelic assistance to minister to Elijah and bring him out of the deep slumber of attack. Jezebel wanted to mute his senses and zap his strength. Prophets are fierce warriors who are wired with a high regard for justice. They tend to see things as right or wrong and refuse to compromise. They are one of the greatest threats to this foul spirit. That is why it will fight them tooth and nail.

Fear Not

It is critical that we realize there is no room for fear or defeat in the kingdom of God. We have been granted all power and authority through the name of Jesus! We are never to shrink back from the enemies of the Lord. We are to get wisdom and strategy to dismantle both the kingdom and powers of hell. Fear not, for the Lord God Almighty fights for you and with you!

> Do not fear, for I am with you; do not be dismayed, for I am your God. I will strengthen you, I will help you, yes, I will uphold you with My righteous right hand.
> —Isaiah 41:10

> Look, I give you authority to trample on serpents and scorpions, and over all the power of the enemy. And nothing shall by any means hurt you.
> —Luke 10:19

While Jezebel is one of the nastiest spirits you will ever encounter, it is vital that you maintain a kingdom perspective on the authority that God has given you. We are to study and discern demons, not to be afraid of them but to be empowered to conquer them. "For we are not ignorant of [Satan's] devices" (2 Cor. 2:11).

We are always to fight these spiritual battles from a position of faith, wisdom, and authority. Faith is empowered by focusing more on the answer than on the current problem. Yes, we know there is an attack, and yes, we know where it is coming from. But we also know where we stand with God. We have the answers. We boldly stand upon the Word of God, unafraid. It is imperative that you keep your mind planted in the Word of God. Don't be moved by Jezebel's evil report. Don't give in to the cloud of confusion that you may be feeling. It all has to bow!

WISDOM IS DERIVED BY TWO METHODS

There are two methods for gaining wisdom. First, wisdom comes from study. Second Timothy 2:15 says, "Study to show yourself approved by God, a workman who need not be ashamed, rightly dividing the word of truth." Becoming a student of God's Word is vital for successful kingdom living. You have to know what God says about you, your current situation, and the intended outcome.

Second, wisdom comes from intimate relationship and encounter with God.

> The Spirit of the LORD shall rest upon him, the Spirit of wisdom and understanding, the Spirit of counsel and might, the Spirit of knowledge and of the fear of the LORD.
>
> —ISAIAH 11:2

The Holy Spirit provides wisdom, counsel, understanding, and ability. You cannot spend time with Holy Spirit and not get insight! He is the Spirit of wisdom. Wisdom unlocks strategy. Strategy is the how-to. You know where you are to go, but you must have a strategy for how to get there. Spiritual warfare demands wise strategy.

> Or what king, going to wage war against another king, does not sit down first and take counsel whether he is able with ten thousand to meet him who comes against him with twenty thousand?
>
> —Luke 14:31

People are often ignorant concerning spiritual warfare. They pick fights without a solid battle plan and end up sidelined by defeat and discouragement. Apostolic people are strategic people. They pray strategic prayers, they implement strategic plans, and they embark on strategic journeys.

You fight by enforcing your authority. Jesus won it all. You are boxing in a match that is fixed. You have been granted the ultimate legal jurisdiction over the enemy. The key is to war from the heavenlies and the place of your authority, not on an equal plane. That is the lie of the enemy, trying to call you down from heavenly places and get you stuck and vulnerable.

> Then Elisha the prophet called one of the sons of the prophets, "Prepare yourself. Take this flask of oil in your hand, and go to Ramoth Gilead. When you get there, look for Jehu the son of Jehoshaphat, the son of Nimshi. Go in and make him rise from among his brothers, and bring him into an inner chamber. Then take the flask of oil, pour it on his head, and say, 'Thus says the LORD: I have anointed you king over Israel.' Then open the door and flee. Do not wait."
>
> So the young man, the prophet, went to Ramoth Gilead. When he arrived, the commanders of the army were sitting, and he said, "I have a word for you, Commander."

Jehu said, "Which one of us?"

And he said, "For you, Commander."

So he arose, went into the house, poured the oil on his head, and said to him, "Thus says the LORD, God of Israel: I am anointing you king over the people of the LORD, over Israel. You will strike the house of Ahab your master, and I will avenge the blood of my servants the prophets and the blood of all the servants of the LORD from the hand of Jezebel. The whole house of Ahab will perish, and I will cut off from Ahab all the males in Israel, both imprisoned and free. I will make the house of Ahab like the house of Jeroboam son of Nebat and like the house of Baasha the son of Ahijah. Dogs will eat Jezebel in the territory of Jezreel, and no one will bury her." Then he opened the door and fled.

—2 KINGS 9:1–10

The word of the Lord came forth powerfully that Jezebel's rule was over. She had resisted God's plan, defiled God's people, and withstood all prophetic correction. She would be killed and consumed by the dogs. Her end would be as violent as her evil reign.

BORN FOR WAR

Prophets and prophetic people are born for war. They are bold, radical, spiritual warriors who see the attacks of the enemy but also see the power that is available for God's people. They do not back down from a fight. Jezebel reigned through terror, witchcraft, seduction, and intimidation, but God's prophet spoke her death sentence. The time was at hand for a deliverance in the kingdom, and her evil witchcraft could not stop it.

Jehu heard the word of the Lord and arose. He got in his chariot and went out for war. He was empowered by the directive of the Almighty. He did not sit in fear, wondering what would happen. What we need in this hour is a Jehu anointing! We need people to arise with the spirit that Jehu had upon him to break demon powers. It takes the spirit of Elijah to expose Jezebel but a Jehu anointing to break the spell. I pray that God raises up Jehus in ministries, in families, in regions, and in nations. May the holy boldness of the Lord be released, and may a supernatural anointing for victorious warfare be poured out upon God's people in this time!

Jehu armed himself for battle. He had the spirit of might upon him as he tapped into the justice of the Lord. We need a mantle of justice on our lives that becomes offended by the trespassing and meddling of Jezebel. We need a boldness to say enough is enough! We must get firm with the powers of hell and say NO to witchcraft over our families, NO to demonic forces in our ministries, and NO to devilish confusion over our minds. A Jehu anointing causes you to rise up in holy boldness and deal with the devil.

The spirit of Elijah recognized, exposed, and confronted Jezebel, but it was Jehu who defeated the witch. The Elijah anointing empowers us to see and expose Jezebel, but we must not stop there. We need the strength, boldness, and power of Jehu to rid our lives of this foul demon.

> When Jehu came to Jezreel, Jezebel heard about it. She put black paint on her eyes, adorned her head, and looked down through the window. As Jehu entered in at the gate, she said, "Is everything all right, Zimri, murderer of his master?"
>
> And he lifted up his face toward the window and said, "Who is on my side? Who?" And two or three eunuchs looked down to him. He said, "Drop her down." So they

dropped her down and some of her blood splattered on the wall and on the horses. Then he trampled her.

Then he entered, ate and drank, and said, "Attend to that cursed woman and bury her, for she is a king's daughter." So they went to bury her, but they found nothing of her except a skull, the feet, and the palms of her hands. They returned and told Jehu, and he said, "This is the word of the Lord, which He spoke by His servant Elijah the Tishbite, saying, 'On the property of Jezreel dogs will eat the flesh of Jezebel. The corpse of Jezebel will be like dung in the field on the property of Jezreel, so that they cannot say, This is Jezebel.'"

—2 Kings 9:30–37

Jezebel attempted one last seduction. She looked out through the window, having painted her eyes and adorned her head. She was hoping to use her seductive powers to escape her execution. Jehu was not entangled in Jezebel's erotic enchantment; instead, he was armed with the word of the Lord and a righteous cause. The Jehu anointing is unafraid of the powers of Jezebel. It is angered by the presence of unholy seduction and offended by bold manipulation.

The anointing upon Jehu brought the fear of the Lord. Those who served Jezebel were suddenly unafraid of her. Those around her who had been in her web of deceit were the very ones who would obey the command of Jehu to throw her down. People often put up with witchcraft and bondage despite repeated warnings from the Lord. They need the bold mantle of Jehu to come and set them free. Jehu did not ask or plead; he demanded justice. "Throw the witch down!" That was his unwavering demand, and in a single moment the demon-possessed queen met her death. She was thrown down, trampled upon, and eaten by the dogs. She was defeated, and the power of her spell, broken.

STRATEGIES TO BREAK
THE HOLD OF A JEZEBEL SPIRIT

- **Discern.** Properly identifying this spirit empowers you to break free from it.

- **Pray.** Warfare requires wisdom. Do not just immediately address it; you will come under counterattack and warfare. Allow the Lord to give you divine wisdom and insight.

- **Establish godly boundaries of authority.** Don't be an Ahab! Jezebel pushes the boundaries, disrespecting all manner of authority. Everything in the kingdom has rank and order. It is a breach of biblical understanding to claim that Holy Spirit is against order and authority. Establish Spirit-led boundaries in your personal life, in your family, and in ministry. Do not be pushed outside of what the Lord has shown you.

- **Use strong spiritual authority.** Demons will laugh at weakness. Fight from a position of strength. Jesus already won the victory! Be like Jehu and make a bold demand. Do not ask demons anything. Cast them out and break their power.

- **Confront, offer repentance, then deliver.** After you have prayed and sought the Lord for clarity, if He has released you to deal with it, then confront the person and the situation. Offer opportunity for growth, repentance, and deliverance. Most people bound with Jezebel refuse to even examine their hearts because they are deeply deceived. If repentance is shunned, then their influence, position, or relationship in your life must be severed.

Typically there will be a power struggle. Be prepared, and know that if you are walking in righteousness and integrity, then the Lord will defend you. Don't be manipulated or moved by the emotional manifestations or spiritual pressure. Stand strong! Stand on the truth! Stand on the Word!

POINTS TO CONSIDER

- » Is there any area in your life where you have taken on an Ahab mentality?

- » Have you allowed a Jezebel spirit to operate?

- » If you discern that Ahab spirit, kick it out. Call forth the fire of God to cleanse and purge.

- » Jezebel and Ahab are codependent and rely on each other.

- » Demons work in packs. Find the leader and kick it out.

- » Do not fear; use your authority.

WHERE TO BEGIN

- » Determine to close any and all doors of manipulation.

- » Refuse to take on an Ahab personality and create illegal agreements in the spirit.

- » Study covenant thinking and living. Be strong and bold.

» Realize that God has boundaries. It is important to honor His ways.

PRAYER

Lord, I thank You that I am a covenant person. Teach me how to live with Your heart and perspective. I refuse to take on an Ahab personality. I thank You that I walk in truth and kingdom identity. I thank You that I take a stand for what is right. You have granted me authority over the powers of hell. I am unafraid of the powers of Jezebel. I thank You that all witchcraft, confusion, and curses of Jezebel are broken over my life in Jesus's name. I boldly declare that I am free through the shed blood of Jesus. I release freedom over my entire family in Jesus's name. Amen.

Chapter 6

PYTHON,
THE HEAT-SEEKING DECEIVER

THERE IS NOTHING like the fresh wind of God blowing upon your life. I can think of so many times I have been in seasons when the refreshing winds of God were blowing. Other times the healing wind of God was blowing. At the first church I planted some years ago, the Lord gave me very specific instructions about conducting a monthly healing meeting. Those meetings became the lifeblood of our young ministry.

The Lord sent people from all over the region and surrounding areas to experience the miracle-working power of God. There was such a wind of God's Spirit on the concept and the gatherings. You could feel God's sense of approval on the direction that we were taking. Of all the things that we had done at the time, those healing meetings were my absolute favorite!

I can vividly remember one evening when a mother brought her teenage son who had major issues with one of his legs. She said he was born with a severe condition that demanded he wear a brace to walk. The mother explained to me that if he attempted to walk without the brace, his leg would just buckle and snap because it lacked the necessary parts to stand. As she shared that with me, I clearly heard the voice of the Lord say to pray and take the brace off. God was going to heal him! I related to the mother what the Lord was prompting me to do.

I wanted her approval and cooperation before taking such a daring step of faith. She agreed. We prayed and took the brace off, and the young man took off running! It was a great day of celebration. God touched his body and caused the impossible to be suddenly possible.

During that season outstanding miracles were commonplace in the meetings. We would get so caught up in the healing presence of God that the miracle realm would just open, and it became easy to get people healed. The ripples from those meetings went out throughout the territory; we became known as a group who believed in miracles. We would frequently receive phone calls asking us to come to the hospital and pray for someone in critical condition. We went and saw wonderful healings and miracles. It was a rich time for our ministry.

Then suddenly the flow in the healing meetings changed. It was as if the life and vitality of the meetings diminished. At first I wondered what we had done to cause this. Was something wrong? Did we grieve Holy Spirit? What was happening? It was clear that the wind was not blowing on these gatherings as strongly as it had been. As I began to pray, the Lord told me that there was a seasonal shift taking place and He wanted to do some new things. He began to pour out strategy. It became clear that the winds of redirection were upon us. As we obeyed the Lord's instructions, we experienced wonderful new assignments, and the hand of God brought even more miracles. The key is that my team and I determined to ride the wind! Wherever the wind of God was blowing, that was where I was going to be. I wasn't going to be out on my own just doing something because it was a good idea.

At this point in my ministry I have experienced so many different seasons. I have had wonderful seasons of pioneering, daring seasons of growth, stunning prophetic seasons of major

God encounters, difficult wilderness seasons of refining, and glorious seasons of revival and renewing. I have also had seasons of rapid advance when God suddenly launched me forward. I have learned to be thankful for each season and have determined to maximize the moment. People who ride the wind refuse to stay stuck! God is not stuck, and He never planned for you to be stuck. When the wind blows upon an area of your life, follow that wind!

> Then the LORD will appear over them, and His arrow will go forth like lightning; and the Lord GOD will blow the trumpet, and will march in the storm winds of the south.
> —ZECHARIAH 9:14, NASB

The Lord spoke to Israel and told them that He would defend them. He said that He would march in the wind and their help was in the wind. Some time ago I was praying and reading about great men and women of God. I found that many of them learned how to ride the winds. They were not so stuck in their ways that they could not change course when heaven mandated it. This is a spirit life key! You must be willing to go where the wind of God is sending you. You cannot just go by your own ideas or thinking. I read about one great revivalist who said that she always kept a bag packed. She would get caught up in the Spirit, and God would tell her to go to a nation, so she would immediately gather her things and head out.[1] God used her to shake nations. She carried His glory in a significant manner and ministered under the glorious winds of heaven.

GLORY IS IN THE WIND

Glory people are Spirit people! Spirit people are wind people; they move with the blowing of the wind of God. They discern the winds of the Spirit. There are various winds of God available to blow on people for various reasons: healing winds, winds of change, winds of transformation, holy winds, and winds of transition.

The Hebrew word for "spirit" is *ruach*, which means "breath" or "wind."[2] Genesis 2:7 says, "Then the LORD God formed man from the dust of the ground and breathed into his nostrils the breath of life, and man became a living being." Notice the order of events: God gathered the dust in order to create mankind, but it was not until the *ruach*, the breath of God and the wind of the Spirit, was released that man lived! The breath of God in us and upon us is what fuels our being. We are a spirit who lives in a body and possesses a soul. We are not a body with a spirit. The essence of who and what we are is the very breath of God Himself.

It was this breath that left Adam and Eve in the garden so that they suddenly died. Their bodies lived, but they were spiritually dead, as they were cursed to be people of the dust and not people of the spirit. The spirit is the life! We are carriers of the winds of heaven. When we pray, wind is released! When we decree, wind is released! When we prophesy, wind is released! When we worship, wind is released! It comes from our inner man, swirls all around us, and then catches us up into heavenly wind.

How did God birth the church? Did He assemble everyone together to be taught theology lessons? Did He begin with an organizational meeting? Did He have a heavenly board meeting to vote on what to do and how to do it? The answer to all these questions is a resounding no!

God urged a hungry people to gather in a room and to wait there. They were to assemble and patiently remain on standby until something miraculous happened. They were asked to believe in something they had never seen or experienced. They were promised something revolutionary and remarkable. They were given the task of prayer. Prayer fuels the arrival and release of the wind in our lives.

As this band of faithful ones was gathered in the Upper Room, there was a suddenly! In a moment, God blew through that assembly with a wild display of His power. The early church was launched in the wind!

> When the day of Pentecost had come, they were all together in one place. Suddenly a sound like a mighty rushing wind came from heaven, and it filled the whole house where they were sitting. There appeared to them tongues as of fire, being distributed and resting on each of them, and they were all filled with the Holy Spirit and began to speak in other tongues, as the Spirit enabled them to speak.
>
> —ACTS 2:1–4

The sound of the wind hit, and everything changed. Holy Spirit showed up in the wind. His breath began to flow through that place, and things were turned upside down. No one was the same. It wasn't a sound effect. They were hearing the entrance of the Spirit of God; the wind had arrived. Tongues broke forth, and fire fell. New wine was poured out as men and women were intoxicated in the glory of God. They left that room forever changed.

Peter, who had denied Christ and was wracked with fear,

became bold as a lion. He had been baptized in the wind and fire. He was chosen by God in a redemptive act to preach the first sermon of the church and to win three thousand people to Jesus in a single moment. The wind that blew that day shifted the course of human history. That same wind is still blowing and rewriting history. That wind is still lifting men and women out of obscurity and mantling them for nations. That same wind is still releasing flames of consuming fire. That same wind is still sweeping gatherings of the hungry and reaching the very deepest places in the hearts of men.

There is a spirit from the depths of hell that hates the wind. It comes to quench the breath and choke its victim to death. It is in the trio of anti-anointing demons that we are revealing in this book. It hides, waiting for the perfect moment to strike and implement its diabolical plans. It is a spirit that is determined to find people and places full of the wind of God and suffocate them.

SOUNDS RIGHT BUT WRONG SPIRIT

The apostle Paul was on a preaching assignment when he encountered this evil demon:

> On one occasion, as we went to the place of prayer, a servant girl possessed with a spirit of divination met us, who brought her masters much profit by fortune-telling. She followed Paul and us, shouting, "These men are servants of the Most High God, who proclaim to us the way of salvation."
>
> —ACTS 16:16–17

Paul was on his way to prayer. He was on assignment, determined to see the gospel released in a powerful capacity. As he was focused on his mission, a great distraction arose. This young woman, who was totally possessed with an evil spirit, began to follow him. She was constantly crying out as she followed him. The content of her message was not wrong, but there was a wicked entity involved in her pursuit.

Paul had arrived in the region with a clear mandate from the Lord to spread the gospel. He was sent as an apostle to bring liberty, truth, and salvation. He was a general deployed into a crucial mission field. Who met him? I believe it was the ruling spirit of that region. I will elaborate as we continue. This young lady followed him and would not relent. She was possessed by a spirit of divination. The literal translation of *divination* is "python."[3] The girl was being controlled by the python spirit. It was binding the region with fortune-telling, incantations, and evil spiritual practices over the land. Paul was there to break its grip, but it was determined to stop him. Paul was being hunted by a serpent!

He wasn't sitting around doing nothing. He was in hot pursuit of God's presence and plan. He was on his way to prayer when this snake showed up. This spirit comes on the scene when a person is full of the life-giving breath of God. To more fully understand the tactics of this spirit, we must recognize the type of serpent a python is.

A python is a fierce, suffocating warrior that quietly and methodically stalks its prey. It does not kill a victim with venom. The danger of the python is not its bite but its strength. When it sinks its teeth into its victim, the python is able to wrap its muscular body around the victim, constricting slowly. As the victim struggles for breath, the python tightens its hold. Every time the victim exhales, the pressure is increased, breaking bones and totally overwhelming the respiratory system. Finally the victim concedes to the massive grip of the serpent, dying of suffocation.

A python kills by removing the breath—this is the picture of this vile spirit.

A python is a heat seeker. It identifies life by locating heat. Dead things are cold, but living things are full of warmth. The python spirit looks for the move of God. It looks for spiritual breakthrough and those pursuing the more. It finds those on their way to higher places and slithers through their lives and ministries, waiting to impose its deadly grasp.

> She did this for many days. But becoming greatly troubled, Paul turned to the spirit and said, "I command you in the name of Jesus Christ to come out of her." And it came out at that moment.
>
> When her masters saw that the hope of their profits was gone, they seized Paul and Silas, and dragged them into the marketplace to the rulers. And they brought them to the magistrates, saying, "These men, being Jews, greatly trouble our city and teach customs which are not lawful for us, being Romans, to receive or observe."
>
> The crowd rose up together against them. And the magistrates tore the garments off them and gave orders to beat them. After they had laid many stripes on them, they threw them into prison, commanding the jailer to guard them securely. Having received such an order, he threw them into the inner prison and fastened their feet in the stocks.
>
> At midnight Paul and Silas were praying and singing hymns to God, and the prisoners were listening to them. Suddenly there was a great earthquake, so that the foundations of the prison were shaken. And immediately all the doors were opened and everyone's shackles were loosened.
>
> —Acts 16:18–26

This young woman persistently followed Paul and his team around. She was loosing evil witchcraft against them. Though her words were not necessarily incorrect, Paul discerned the spirit behind what she was saying. This is how the devil works—when you are pressing in to the fire of God, the passion of prayer, and the longing for revival, the enemy sends a demonic attack to distract and disrupt your pursuit.

Paul was grieved in his spirit. He could sense the presence of evil in this young lady. On the outside it may have looked good, but there was a foul serpent lurking just beneath the surface. Thank God for the discerning of spirits and revelation knowledge. If only all Christians realized what a powerful position they occupy in the spirit through the completed work of Jesus. Not only did Jesus win the spiritual battles for us and position us in Him, but He also paved the way for the wonderful Holy Spirit to come and indwell us. We can hear from heaven and avoid devilish traps through the leading of the Spirit. Galatians 5:25 says, "If we live in the Spirit, let us also walk in the Spirit." We can walk with Holy Spirit into truth, illumination, and victory! We do not have to be blinded by the powers of hell.

The python spirit is connected to fortune-telling and the working of familiar spirits. This young lady brought great financial rewards to her masters through her fortune-telling. She was empowered by a false spirit. The Greeks believed in the connection between Python and Apollo. They also embraced an "oracle," a demon-possessed false prophet whose body would be taken over by familiar spirits to release the utterances provided from evil spirits. The Greeks believed wholeheartedly in these evil spiritual practices.

This culture of a python and the oracle predicting events had invaded Philippi. This evil python spirit and its practices influenced everyday life in Macedonia. According to Greek mythology, the serpent, who guarded the temple at Delphi, was killed by Apollo (and then the oracle at Delphi took on the name Pythia, and Apollo became known as Pythian Apollo).[4] The word Pythian was later applied to diviners or soothsayers inspired by Apollo.[5] The python spirit empowers evil sorceries and false spirit communication. As Paul was ministering throughout the region of Macedonia, he undoubtedly saw and discerned the reach and grip of this evil spirit.

There are historical accounts of violent physical reactions as false prophetic voices yielded to this demon in Greek culture and released utterances.[6] Their bodies were overtaken by this serpent. In much the same way as the power of God affected people's physical bodies in the Upper Room, this demonic entity overwhelms a person who opens the door and creates evil manifestations as it releases its venomous prophecies.

The python spirit is alive and well in the world today, working through psychics, fortune-tellers, mediums, and all manner of false spiritualists. These underworld practices are clearly and strongly forbidden in the Bible. Leviticus 20:6 states, "The person who turns to spirits through mediums and necromancers in order to whore after them, I will even set My face against that person and will cut him off from among his people." Christians are not to seek out spiritual assistance from any source other than God's Word, His gifts, His Spirit, and those being led by His Spirit. Seeking spiritual assistance elsewhere is a sure way to open doors to the enemy in your life.

A number of years ago I encountered a woman who was totally overrun with demonic powers. She would sit in church meetings and begin to manifest demons. Her body would contort in a way that looked as if a serpent was operating through her. As the process unfolded, she would twitch with strange movements and then belch repeatedly.

The manifestations became a tremendous distraction. The leaders at the church were ministering to her, but she refused spiritual help. She would have to be removed from meetings because of the commotion she would cause. I will never forget one episode in church. There was a guest speaker preaching quite powerfully. In the blink of an eye, the demon-possessed woman turned and slapped her husband across the face. It made a huge noise, and everyone looked around, but she had moved under supernatural power, and very few people saw it because it was so fast. I happened to catch it from where I was sitting, but she moved uncommonly fast.

This woman had gotten wrapped up in false spiritual practices and became overwhelmed by the power of darkness. She opened a door for demons to come inhabit her. The devil doesn't care how small the crack in the door is—he will exploit it to come in. This is why governing our spiritual lives by the Word of God and obeying the promptings of Holy Spirit are critical.

The python spirit seeks to ensnare people in a false prophetic capacity, to choke the very life of God out of them. The python spirit will release false fire over your life. The python spirit will release false words over your future. The python spirit will loose strange fire upon you. The python spirit will entice you and then cunningly take you into its deadly lair to defeat you.

Vision Invader

One of the words for "prophet" in the Old Testament is translated "seer" (e.g., 2 Sam. 24:11). The Scriptures often refer to Old Testament prophets as seers. This is a particular type of prophetic function that indicates a high level of visionary encounters in the realm of the spirit. Seers receive detailed prophetic encounters in visions, dreams, and night visions. They process the realm of the spirit in high definition. They are often totally swept up into the spirit realm, far beyond the confines of this natural world. They feel and sense things in a way that is deeply impacting. This is true of all prophetic people. They are extremely engaged in the realm of the spirit.

Many young prophets and seers struggle to find anyone who can assist them in developing their gift, to understand the very real experiences they are having. Oftentimes churches shun the prophetic ministry due to lack of understanding, controlling demons, or religious traditions. It's sad to say, but many churches today have made a conscious decision to program out the move of God. They view prophets and prophetic people as troublemakers.

These abandoned prophets in the making are having spiritual encounters and experiences that they don't understand. If they cannot find help in the kingdom of God, they can be drawn into false spiritual practices because they are embraced by people who have spiritual language and an understanding of what they are experiencing. Sadly I believe that many God-called prophets have been deceived by the python spirit and are functioning outside of God's call and blessing upon their lives. This is one reason that I am passionate about prophetic teaching, training, and activation. I don't want to see python tangle up and deceive future world changers.

I pray that God will raise up an army of spiritual mothers and fathers who will accept, love, and groom prophets, seers, and those with uncommon prophetic abilities. It is also key that those being trained are humble and submissive. One of the quickest ways for a deeply prophetic person to get off track is pride. Seeing and knowing in the spirit realm is a God-given gift. Pride comes in when people begin to use their gifts as a means of lifting themselves up and demanding people recognize their greatness. It becomes very demonic behavior that draws people away from Jesus and does damage to the people of God instead of strengthening them and serving them.

> Pride goes before destruction, and a haughty spirit before a fall.
>
> —PROVERBS 16:18

The python spirit comes to choke the life, the wind, and the breath out of you. When you are under attack from a python spirit, there is an uncommon sense of heaviness and oppression. As much as it is a false prophetic spirit, it is also a wicked spirit of bondage. It was no mistake that it was attempting to distract and derail the apostle Paul. It wanted to stall out the mission that God had sent him on. It wanted to abort the apostolic assignment. Python comes to rob the life-giving force of anointing and power.

In *The Spiritual Warfare Battle Plan*, Jennifer LeClaire sums it up perfectly:

> The python spirit had a stronghold in Philippi. When the man of prayer started heading for the house of prayer, this spirit launched its first attack against him—a distraction followed by a full-blown trial that aimed to take him out of his purpose. Python knows it has no authority in a city that prays in the presence of God, so it works to distract people from praying so they can't fulfill their purpose.
>
> Python would rather watch you lick your wounds than pray to a healing God. Python would rather hear you complain or gossip than take your problems to a miracle-working God. Python would rather distract you

with attacks, trials, and persecutions than see you press into a gracious God for deliverance. Again, python's ultimate goal is to put you in bondage and thwart your purpose. You may be going through the motions but feel dead on the inside because python has squeezed the life out of you.[7]

The python spirit is an enemy of revival! It shows up to squeeze those who are pressing in to receive fresh flames of fire, strong anointing, and life-giving outpouring. Python has an assignment in regions to clearly identify those who pose a spiritual threat. When new ministries are established in a lukewarm territory and begin to engage the heavenlies, releasing the life of God over dry people, python senses the heat and comes lurking in the darkness, ready to strike. Understanding the operation of this spirit is essential for those who are going to shake a territory. It is certain that python will show up. Recognizing its evil plots empowers you to overcome.

The python spirit comes into families to put them under such a heavy squeeze that they quit moving forward. There is an anointing for families. In the same way that God empowers a person for exploits or a church for great things, He can release fresh oil over a family to bond together, to love one another, to experience the kingdom together, and to defeat the operation of hell. Python will come to bind up that power and create a cold atmosphere void of the life of God.

Python comes against prayer. This spirit wants to kill prayer lives. It knows that prayer is one of the most potent weapons in the arsenal of a believer. It doesn't mind if people go through the motions of religion with no spiritual power, but when they begin to hunger for intimate communication with God, this demon gets nervous. Paul was raising up a kingdom movement that centered on prayer and the presence of God, and python was determined to shut it down. If Paul had not properly discerned this demon, it is hard to say where the church would be today. Thank God the apostle of God refused to give in. Thank God he didn't move away from the promise. Thank God he rebuked that demon. Thank God he was a warrior.

Points to consider

- » Have you been distracted, particularly in prayer?
- » Have you opened any doors to familiar spirits?
- » Have you battled heaviness?
- » Do you feel as if you just cannot go forward in what God has called you to do?
- » Are there any enduring spiritual battles that could be the operation of a python spirit?

Where to begin

- » Understand that the python spirit comes after things that are alive.
- » When you press in to God, this demon will attempt to take you out.
- » Concerning prophetic ministry, it is extremely important to guard yourself, making sure that you are drinking from a pure stream. How can you know that? By a person's fruit, alignments, and integrity.
- » Don't just accept every prophetic word; examine it by the written Word, and make sure the vessel is pure. This does not mean to be critical, but it

means to honestly evaluate. Deception begins with a small seed.

PRAYER

I thank You, Lord, that I am not deceived. I hear Your voice and obey Your leading. I ask for clear direction. Lord, I come before You, thanking You for Your purity in my life. I receive the washing of Your blood, and I thank You for freedom from all deception. I embrace Your wind in my life! I am hungry for Your anointing, for Your power, for Your fire! I want Your life moving in me and ministering to others through me. I break the grip of every operation of the python spirit in Jesus's name. I break its power right now and command it to go! I thank You, Lord, that I am free indeed. In Jesus's name, amen.

Chapter 7

BREAKING PYTHON'S GRIP

W E'VE ESTABLISHED THAT the python spirit attacks and chokes the breath out of its victims. When Paul exposed this spirit, it was hiding in a young lady. She was saying and doing things that seemed right to others, yet there was something that disturbed Paul. He was looking beyond the natural realm, glimpsing the unseen realm of spirits. One of the keys to defeating this spirit is recognition. You must be able to see it to defeat it.

KNOW YOUR ENEMY

The gift of discerning of spirits empowers a believer to see the spirit motivating a person or situation. During the operation of this gift, spiritual eyes are opened so that truth is illuminated. This is imperative in dealing with the enemy, who is a master at hiding. Prophetic exposure brings violent confrontation.

When Paul cast the python spirit out, there was a massive counterattack, but his faith never wavered. After being attacked, mistreated, and falsely accused, he held a spontaneous worship service in a prison cell. His praise brought about liberty.

Paul's reaction reveals keys to freedom from this spirit: worship, praise, and faith. We will explore each of these keys to understand how they bring deliverance from the grip of an evil serpent. We will also examine the appearance of demonic spirits throughout the Bible and the promises of God's power over their attacks. We will draw lessons from the life of Paul by discussing his demonic encounters and victory strategies.

To grasp the concept of the python spirit, it is important to identify the hunting techniques of an actual python. These serpents are not known to kill their prey with deadly venom. They hide, lurking in the darkness and patiently waiting to capture their victim. They are proficient in identifying life by the presence of heat. Where there is heat, there is vitality and breath. As we established earlier, breath represents life in the spirit and the move of God. A python spirit, then, comes after that which is alive and moving. It has no interest in stalking lukewarm believers—they are already in its grip. It comes after people who are manifesting the heat of God and releasing the breath of heaven. It lies in wait for the perfect moment to strike.

When does python strike? As a person is pressing in to the things of God. This demon stalked the apostle Paul on his way to prayer. Its purpose was to extinguish the move of God. A python spirit suddenly strikes its prey, coiling its massive body around the victim, putting it in a deadly squeeze, and slowly killing it. This demon functions much like a natural python in that it grips its victim, choking the spiritual wind out of it.

The python spirit hates the life-giving anointing of God and comes to contaminate, diminish, and quench the anointing. It is hunting every person who is moving in the Spirit. It is on the prowl, looking for fiery places of revival, with the intent of shutting down the move of God. It is actively searching the earth for ministries that are moving in the Spirit. It will release plans to stall out the move of God.

When the python spirit strikes, vitality is lost, and the life of God is suffocated. It loves to choke out the move of God. It loves to remove the life-giving flow of heaven. Under attack by a python spirit, you feel lifeless. It squeezes you with fierce pressure to get you to give up on hopes, dreams, plans, and purposes. It wants you to settle for a mediocre spiritual life void of the rich power of heaven.

The python spirit will get you second-guessing the things that heaven clearly and accurately revealed to you in the secret place. This is one of the cornerstones of a python attack. It grips the mind and does all that it can to stall out your pursuit of heaven's agenda. It is an anti-anointing demon. The anointing is connected to purpose. Python is on assignment to dilute your purpose and thereby hinder the anointing in your life.

Heavy mind traffic and swirling thoughts of confusion are elements of the python attack plan. The enemy knows that the mind is the point of logic, thought, and reason. If he can sow seeds of destruction and confusion in the human mind, then he can create questioning of the call of God, stealing clarity.

> I will set no wicked thing before my eyes. I hate the work
> of those who turn aside; it shall not have part of me.
> —PSALM 101:3

This is a strong word! Guarding our eyes ultimately helps protect our minds. The enemy recognizes the power of the human mind. It has often been said that if you can imagine it, you can become it. The Bible declares in Proverbs 23:7 that as a man thinks in his heart, so is he. This means that our inner thought life dictates the direction of our outward living. When a spiritual attack strikes the mind, the ultimate goal is to pollute thinking and cause the person to sink down into a pit of despair. This is especially true when the python spirit is at work. Its twisting and deceitful lies put purpose under siege in an attempt to derail destiny.

Therefore guard your minds, be sober, and hope to the
end for the grace that is to be brought to you at the revelation of Jesus Christ.

—1 Peter 1:13

We are to be intentional about guarding our thought lives.
We cannot and must not allow every negative thought to take
root in our imaginations. Our imaginations are the creative
engines of our beings. When our imaginations are not protected, we begin to see, dream, and declare destruction. The aim
of a spiritual attack is to get people so bound in confusion and
fear that they prophesy their own defeat.

Python Pollutes

A python spirit overwhelms its prey with a barrage of negative
thoughts. It attempts to pollute the creative flow with damaging
negativity. We must be quick to recognize this scheme, casting
down contrary thoughts with the name of Jesus and the Word
of God as two of our weapons. In 2 Corinthians 10:5 we are
instructed to cast down imaginations. This is not passive on our
parts. This is aggressive warfare. This demands action from us.
In the spirit realm words carry authority and power. We must
combat the lies of the enemy with a strong confession. We need
to immediately command those thoughts to leave in the name
of Jesus. We must exercise bold authority over lying thoughts
with the words of our mouths.

Whoever guards his mouth and his tongue keeps his soul
from trouble.

—Proverbs 21:23

Keeping our mouths full of the Word of God, the promises
of God, and the will of God is the key to victory. We are to

combat the lies of the enemy with the words of our mouths. We are also to use the Word of God as a weapon. For every lie, we need to answer with a truth. Answer the attack with a promise. Jesus revealed a tremendously effective warfare strategy when the devil came to tempt Him. Each time the enemy released warfare and lies against Him, He answered with the Word of God.

> Then Jesus said to him, "Get away from here, Satan! For it is written, 'You shall worship the Lord your God, and Him only shall you serve.'"
> —MATTHEW 4:10

The devil hurled lies and temptations at Jesus, but at every point he was met with truth. Jesus stood on the Word of God. Jesus spoke the Word of God. Jesus fought the devil with the Word of God. This is our example when under attack—we need to meet the enemy with the Word of God. God's Word acts as a defensive weapon, repelling the aggressive advances of the enemy. We can stand firmly upon the promises in the Word of God. As we dive deep into God's Word, our faith is built, and we are empowered to come out of the crippling effect of spiritual attack.

When the apostle Paul discerned, confronted, and cast out the python spirit, there was an uproar. Paul and Silas were brutally attacked, stripped, beaten, and imprisoned as a result of a major demonic counterattack. Demons and demonic powers understand the art of war. One of the things that a successful army must do is stop the advance of the enemy. The army cannot allow an advance to go forth without opposing it. Many times when you engage the realm of the spirit and catch the attention of the enemy, you will receive a counterattack. Knowing this prepares you to face the onslaught and come out on the other side with victory. You are not to have a spirit of fear; you are to become a skillful warrior.

> He trains my hands for war, so that my arms bend a bow of bronze. You have given me the shield of Your salvation, and Your right hand has held me up, and Your gentleness has made me great.
> —PSALM 18:34–35

David penned this powerful declaration of strength. He was known as a fierce warrior who understood the art of battle and had tasted the sweet cup of victory. Time and again God delivered and defended this radical lover of His presence. David was a worshipping warrior. He knew how to hide deeply in the arms of the Father. His unwavering affection for the Lord brought the presence of God into his life like a tidal wave. He dwelled in the courts of the Lord, enjoying immeasurable favor and supernatural protection. He faced massive spiritual attacks but kept coming out on the other side with the victory.

USE YOUR SECRET WEAPONS

The journey into destiny is not completed without a fight. The python spirit comes to undo the sense of purpose in our lives. It comes to squeeze out the fresh breath of heaven. It comes to hinder our prayer lives and dilute the anointing we carry. Python launched a severe retaliation against Paul and his apostolic team, but they had a secret weapon.

> At midnight Paul and Silas were praying and singing hymns to God, and the prisoners were listening to them. Suddenly there was a great earthquake, so that the foundations of the prison were shaken. And immediately

all the doors were opened and everyone's shackles were loosened.

—ACTS 16:25–26

Despite the unjust beatings, the public humiliation they faced by being stripped naked in front of everyone, and their imprisonment, Paul and Silas decided to lift their voices in praise at the midnight hour. It is revealing that they began their spontaneous worship session at the darkest time of night. There is a message here. When the enemy blasts or retaliates against you and everything is falling apart, praise will bring you supernatural strength. Praise is a weapon!

When we enter the realm of praise, we are fervently expressing our gratitude to the Lord and remembering His greatness. Praise establishes Jesus as Lord over every trial, every storm, every attack, and every present circumstance in our lives. As we fill our mouths with thanksgiving and fervent declarations of the goodness of God, we break through the fog of battle and encounter the warmth of His love and the force of His power. In 2 Chronicles 20 the men of Judah supernaturally won the battle against the enemy by praising and worshipping God. God defended them and set ambushes against their enemies because of their affection for Him. Praise was the choice weapon!

It was Paul's and Silas's praise that brought the presence of God into the prison and shook them loose. Praise can break the chains of bondage. Praise can shatter the lies of the enemy. Praise can chip away at the heaviness and release the glory. Once the glory comes in, you cannot stay bound. It is impossible. When God's presence fills a place, bondage has no choice but to go. Praise brings liberty.

I remember a time when the power of God was healing people as I was ministering in a small church. A man came forward who had been battling severe back pain and had very limited movement. I felt the anointing and the power of God as I began to pray for him. After I prayed, I asked him to check his movement and the pain. Nothing had changed as far as he could tell. I began to praise the Lord. As I thanked God and worshipped Him, I got totally swept up in His presence. I was getting so blessed by the presence of God that I really forgot about the man and our prayer request. My hands were still on the man because I had been praying for him, but now I was lost in the presence of God, having my own praise party. After several minutes a surge of God's anointing came. The man began to move, and he said he was without pain and had full restoration of movement. Praise had overtaken affliction!

DISCERNING A PYTHON ATTACK

There are two ways that you can properly detect the presence of a python spirit. First, you can identify it by becoming aware of its tactics. Secondly, it can be supernaturally revealed to you through the gifts of the Spirit. We will discuss both methods, but we will begin by listing the symptoms of a python attack and exploring each one to be equipped to detect, confront, and defeat this slithering demon.

It comes on the scene during a spiritual advance.

The python spirit shows up in the life of a person during his or her pursuit of God. Python comes on the scene in the life of a church or ministry as it is pressing in to the deeper things of God. Python has an assignment to bind and hinder the anointing. It is drawn to Holy Spirit heat. This attack will come at times of spiritual movement and progress.

It says things that sound right but grieve you on the inside.

We do not have a clear record of exactly how this demonic stalker was acting around Paul, but we do know what she was saying. This account provides us with some keen insight. In judging spiritual things, it is vital to examine not only the content but also the spiritual motivation behind it. For example, a minister can preach a sermon on faithfulness, but if his motive is to control people, then it is in error. A person with a python spirit manifesting may say all types of things that are right biblically but does not have a right spirit behind him. If you have a check in your spirit, pay attention. Stop and pray over it. Do not just shun the warning that God is giving you. Paul saw what others could not see.

It makes you feel restricted, overwhelmed, and bound.

All spiritual attacks will release heaviness and bondage upon your life. One of the telltale signs of an attack is when you experience extreme heaviness. The python spirit coils around you and puts you in a tight squeeze. You feel absolutely restricted and bound.

It can come with flattery.

The woman following Paul was saying all types of nice things with an undertone of flattery. Demons will often attempt to gain access by telling us what we want to hear. Again, this is why examination and prayer are key. Flattery overemphasizes things with an ulterior motive. It produces exaggerated kindness and grandiose spiritual announcements. It is designed to entangle your soul in order to get a foothold.

It is a stalker of the anointing.

The python pursues the anointing. It will follow people who are anointed. It will show up in places where there is a strong flow of heaven.

It can partner with religious spirits, the Jezebel spirit, witchcraft, and other demons to twist and squeeze the life out.

Demons like to tag-team and partner for dark conquests. Typically when a major attack is launched against a leading ministry or person, there is more than one hidden devil. A python spirit can work in tandem with a religious spirit to squeeze the power out of someone's life. It can also act with a spirit of witchcraft and Jezebel to manifest a false and contaminated spiritual flow.

It persecutes the function and flow of anointing and comes against the move of God.

When python comes to squeeze out the flow of heaven, it will persecute and mock the anointing of God. If it comes into a ministry, it will come against strong moves of God, finding fault and complaining. It will do the same in someone's personal life. It will bring railing accusation about spiritual encounters. We should and must judge all things by the Word of God, including heavenly encounters. Python raises unfounded concerns to totally shut down the sweet presence of God.

It is drawn to people with the fire of God.

Python looks for those with the flames of God on their lives. It comes to put out the flame. It does not want the people of God burning with cleansing fire.

It is one of the spirits that fuel false prophetic flow, psychics, and so on.

Python empowers occult activity, false predictions, false prophetic flow, and psychic powers. It is an evil demon that manifests false fire. It can accurately relay information that it unlawfully obtains from the spirit realm, but it is totally demonic. It cannot reveal the heart of God. False prophetic ministry always reveals things, details, and pieces of information, but it does not reveal Jesus. Real prophets reveal Jesus! They may share pieces of information or identify something that has happened in your life. Prophets see and know. They hear and encounter. They have supernatural access and can be highly accurate in their prophetic words over our lives, but each and every prophetic encounter will always end up drawing a person closer to Jesus. That is what real prophetic ministry does; anything less than that is false.

It can attempt to access position through impure prophetic ministry.

This is a common attribute of demonic spirits manifesting false fire. They will often attempt to gain an audience with a leader or access into the life of a person with impure prophetic ministry. The python spirit manifests in this capacity looking for influence. It will release information and illegitimate words to bait a person into allowing it into his circle of influence. Authentic prophetic ministry and prophets do not struggle to be noticed or to gain position. Many prophets would rather be in their prayer closets seeking God than on a stage or occupying a position of influence.

It manifests a false anointing and power.

The python spirit can be a carrier of strange fire. It can manifest realms of supernatural power and flow that come from the demonic realm.

It can attack your physical body.

As we know, man is a three-part being. We are a spirit, we live in a body, and we have a soul (mind, will, and emotions). Spiritual attacks typically show up on multiple fronts in these various dimensions of our lives. For example, it is not uncommon for someone under an attack of heaviness to experience physical symptoms of exhaustion. The python spirit is a constrictive spirit that comes to choke off the flow of wind and air. In the spiritual sense it will choke fresh life, prophetic anointing, and Holy Spirit wind. In the physical arena it can manifest as choking, severe respiratory problems, or even coiling of the physical body when being cast out. Many times in deliverance a python spirit being confronted will manifest with serpentlike moves in the physical body. I have seen many prophets and prophetic people get hit with the python spirit and have extraordinary bouts of respiratory, breathing, and throat attacks. These are uncommon attacks with a twofold purpose to manifest in both the spiritual and natural realm. To be clear—not every physical issue is a spirit, but some are! We know that demonic powers can attack the physical realm, and this one does. It attacks the breath, wind, lungs, and voice.

Learning the schemes and operations of the python spirit empowers believers for victory. We can quickly detect its operation and develop a prayer strategy to counteract its unlawful operations. Being armed with proper knowledge brings advantage in the arena of spiritual warfare. As we grow in our understanding of demonic spirits, their wicked desires, their battle tactics, and how to defeat them, we are skillfully equipped for victory.

USE THE GIFTS

Gaining knowledge regarding the python spirit is only one way that we can be prepared. There is another vital tool in uncovering hidden demonic powers. The realm of Spirit leading and the gifts of the Spirit are power weapons to properly expose demon spirits.

Every Christian has the right to tap into the realm of revelation and the leading of Holy Spirit. One of the wonderful gifts that has been provided in this set of gifts is the discerning of spirits.

> But the manifestation of the Spirit is given to everyone for the common good. To one is given by the Spirit the word of wisdom, to another the word of knowledge by the same Spirit, to another faith by the same Spirit, to another gifts of healings by the same Spirit, to another the working of miracles, to another prophecy, to another discerning of spirits, to another various kinds of tongues, and to another the interpretation of tongues. But that one and very same Spirit works all these, dividing to each one individually as He will.
> —1 CORINTHIANS 12:7–11

Believers have been granted unlimited access to the realm of revelation and the all-knowing mind of Christ. Included in the ministry of Holy Spirit are these nine gifts that access spiritual breakthroughs and supernatural power. One of the greatest weapons against hidden devils is the discerning of spirits.

What precisely is the gift of discerning of spirits? It is the ability to see, discern, and recognize the spirit motivating a person or situation. This gift can manifest in a variety of ways. All spiritual gifts operate as a means of transmitting divine information and power. Each one accesses different parts of the nature of God. The discerning of spirits allows a person to see and recognize a spirit being. This gift provides much-needed spiritual intelligence. It can function in a variety of ways. For example, people can discern a spirit by having an inner vision in which they see something with the eyes of their spirit and know that it is a spiritual being. People can experience a scent—they actually smell something that reveals the presence of a demon. In the realm of the spirit, demons are foul! I have had experiences dealing with a person with an unclean spirit when I supernaturally smelled an awful stench that let me know there was a demonic power in operation. People can hear the voice of the Lord speaking to them about a spirit in operation. There are many methodologies of communicating the information, but the end result is the same—a spirit being is revealed.

Every Christian needs to thank God for the nine gifts of the Spirit. When I was first born again, one of my mentors taught me that the Holy Ghost lives in my belly, and therefore all nine gifts of the Spirit live in me. My mentor also told me that if I forgot to claim them, they would not be in operation. Faith is in the believing, speaking, and doing. All exploits of faith have those three components. You believe, and therefore you speak; as you speak, you do! Faith creates movement and momentum.

Spiritual gifts need to be activated. Begin to claim the discerning of spirits in your life. Take time to thank God and tell Him that you believe this gift is in you and active. Speak it out by faith. Then be quick to pay attention when God speaks. One encounter with the discerning of spirits can literally save you years of trouble.

Recently I went to speak for a pastor whom I did not know very well. Right before I was scheduled to go, a dear friend of mine gave me a warning about the pastor and the ministry, but it was too late for me to cancel. When I arrived, I immediately sensed something was not right. The pastor was saying all the right words, but there was a void in the realm of the spirit. I prayed throughout my time there, and my eyes were opened to see a stronghold of rejection that caused the pastor to do immature, even offensive, things. Rejection, control, and even lying manifested while I was there. The discerning of spirits, along with wisdom from understanding spiritual warfare and people, helped me avoid a long-term relationship with this pastor that would have only brought great distraction and damage. I felt bad for the pastor, the church, and the family because they were all hurting as a result of these spirits buffeting this leader. The pastor needed deliverance and emotional healing. Although I was thrilled to minister to the people there, the alignment was bad, and I was glad to get out of that atmosphere. When you are in a spiritually toxic atmosphere, it depletes you. If you are a prophetic person, you really feel the swirling of evil powers, and your heart yearns for deliverance and healing for those involved.

A strategy is an action plan with specific steps to achieve an objective. Let's talk about a strategy to conquer the python spirit in your life, your ministry, your family, or any other facet of daily living. How can we conquer this intruding force?

First, it begins with recognition. All spiritual warfare is rooted in the ability to see what is trying to remain hidden. When you are dealing with any demon, you must see it for what it is. You cannot downplay it or ignore it. Ignoring a demon power in your life can result in horrific consequences. Recognition and identification are critical. Look at the symptoms and the manifestations, and then tap into any leading that you have, but if you are not forced into a timeline, then wait on the Lord for instruction.

Python struck Paul on the way to prayer. Prayer is the force that often unravels the mind of God in a situation. We are given a powerful war strategy in the book of Ephesians, chapter 6, as Paul teaches on the armor of God. No spiritual warrior is complete without armor. Many of us have memorized and know the symbolism behind each piece. We pray and put on our armor by faith. But there is a vital instruction right after the portion of Scripture about our armor. Paul makes a statement that must not be overlooked:

> Pray in the Spirit always with all kinds of prayer and supplication. To that end be alert with all perseverance and supplication for all the saints.
>
> —EPHESIANS 6:18

Spend time praying and listening. It is amazing what God can show you when you seek Him. Prayer is the foundation of productive warfare. Then use your authority! Command the spirit of python to break its hold in the name of Jesus. Paul directly confronted the spirit and cast it out. Command python to go. Stand boldly in the place of authority through the sacrifice of Jesus, and tell the python it has to go. Break its power with the name of Jesus. Break its heaviness with the name of Jesus. Break its divination with the name of Jesus. If python has made any false decrees over you, break them. Take authority over them, and call them broken.

Use the weapon of praise. What did Paul do? He praised God. He boldly lifted his voice to the Lord. Praise will keep the momentum going. If you feel that serpent slithering, twisting, and attacking, start praising God. As you are praising Him, remember the times in your life when His goodness prevailed, and then thank the Lord for them. Get swept up in the goodness of God, and the anointing will flow! When the anointing flows, it will begin smashing the burdens and removing the bondage.

Finally stand upon the Word of God. Follow in the footsteps of Jesus and use the written Word as your promise book. Find key verses that minister to your situation, meditate on them, and then speak them out of your mouth. Answer the enemy with the Word of God! He cannot defeat you when you align yourself with the Word, the blood, and the name of Jesus. Those are victory master keys. Cut off the head of the python and go free.

POINTS TO CONSIDER

> » Have you been discouraged, overwhelmed, or stagnant?

> » Recognize that the python spirit wants to choke out the life in you.

> » Increasing your prayer life will keep you built up in the Spirit.

WHERE TO BEGIN

> » Praise and worship are keys to overcoming any demonic attack.

> » You have authority over demons, so fight back from a place of victory.

> » Jesus taught us to use the Word of God: "It is written."

PRAYER

Thank You, Lord, that I am free from all the power of the enemy. Show me any areas of my life or ministry where I have allowed any demonic influence. Show me if I am compromising in any area, and help me walk in purity and holiness. I decree that I will fulfill the purpose for which I was created and will not be stopped or hindered by the spirit of python or any other spirit. In Jesus's name, amen.

Chapter 8

THE DNA OF THE RELIGIOUS SPIRIT

ONE OF THE ultimate aims of anti-anointing spirits is to trap a person in dead works with no spiritual power or thrust. The anointing is like wind that empowers and accelerates the purposes of God. It is jet fuel in the realm of the spirit. Building in the kingdom without the presence of the anointing will lead to discouragement and bondage. The enemy wants to create a dry spiritual climate with no breakthrough or freedom. One of his favorite weapons is the religious spirit.

What exactly is a religious spirit? Simply defined, it is a demon power that uses religious structures to entangle people in bondage, prevent transformation, and enforce the spiritual status quo. It fights revelation, defies prophetic insight, hates apostolic authority, and uses tradition to build structures of limitation.

DON'T LET THE OIL RUN DRY!

Living in the kingdom demands the precious oil of Holy Spirit on a regular basis. This was one of the most distinguishing aspects of Jesus's ministry. Everywhere He went, there were supernatural results. You could not encounter the ministry of Jesus without encountering the power of God. The two went hand in hand. Hebrews 13:8 boldly declares, "Jesus Christ is the same yesterday, and today, and forever." That means we should expect the same realm of power to show up now when we preach and declare Jesus and His glorious kingdom. The power of God is a witness to the person of Jesus. The power of God is part of the authenticity of the kingdom. The power of God is evidence of our sonship and position of redemption through the blood of the Lamb. We have been granted power over the devil. We have been given supernatural power over disease. We have been given power over temporary circumstances and challenges. Our inheritance brings access to the full majesty of heaven.

We are called to live in the anointing. We are called to move in the supernatural. We should not bow to the lies of the enemy or just give up in defeat. There is oil to help in every situation. There is Holy Spirit power and refreshing. The religious spirit comes to void those realities and crush life in the spirit. It comes to stifle and hinder. It comes to mock and challenge. It comes to bind and restrict.

Many people begin with vibrant spiritual lives but end up dry and empty because of the religious spirit. Some years ago the Lord sent me to a specific region to establish ministries and labor for awakening. We began to experience explosive results. God did spectacular and supernatural things in our midst. After a period of time I began to meet some of the pastors who had sizeable ministries in the region. I noticed a common thread: they were all dry. I heard story after story of how their ministries began with the raw power of God, but over time they were worn down by criticism, complaints, and attacks, only to retreat and build ministries that were lukewarm. As I stepped into a higher perspective, I realized that I was seeing the stronghold in that region—the religious spirit. It was active in every fiber of people's thinking and ruled the churches. It manifested through the sound of the region. It manifested through the government of the region. It manifested through the ekklesia of the region. Any ministry or voice that came in to challenge it was swiftly opposed. Over a period of years I tangled with this spirit many times. I had several prophetic dreams about the religious spirit and its plans in the territory. The bottom line is that it had established a successful stronghold and was choking the life out of the people of God. That is the aim of this horrendous demon.

> Then the Pharisees went and took counsel to entangle Him in His words. They sent their disciples to Him with the Herodians, saying, "Teacher, we know that You are truthful and teach the way of God truthfully, and are swayed by no one. For You do not regard the person of men. Tell us then, what do You think? Is it lawful to pay taxes to Caesar, or not?"
>
> But Jesus perceived their wickedness and said, "Why test Me, you hypocrites? Show Me the tax money." They brought Him a denarius. He said to them, "Whose is this image and inscription?"
>
> They said to Him, "Caesar's."
>
> Then He said to them, "Render therefore to Caesar the things that are Caesar's, and to God the things that are God's."
>
> When they heard these words, they were amazed, and left Him and went on their way.
>
> —MATTHEW 22:15–22

The religious elite of the day were trying to ensnare Jesus in a demonic trap. They were furious because He was preaching a message of power, love, and the kingdom. They were preaching a message of defeat, condemnation, and bondage. Jesus was loosing the captives and delivering the bound. They were exalting themselves while trampling upon the destiny of sons and daughters. Jesus was moving in great power and authority while they were dry and void of breakthrough. This is a picture of the stark contrast between the gospel and religion. The gospel will always point humanity to the grace of the Cross and the complete sacrifice of Jesus. By moving through that reality, we can ultimately find our positions as sons and daughters, demonstrating the kingdom, relating to God as Abba (our Father), and enjoying the carefree life of one who has been gloriously ransomed. It is easy to move in the power of God when we know our roles in His kingdom. Religion preaches a message of death, destruction, and entanglement. Religion strives without results. It points to human weakness instead of divine solutions. Religion works aggressively to deny and nullify the absolute price that was paid at Calvary. Religion continues to demand more without acknowledging that the price has been paid. Religion builds walls instead of doors and gates. Freedom will always offend religion.

In the passage in Matthew 22 there are some telltale signs of the religious spirit. These markers help us properly understand the makeup of this evil power.

They conspired against Jesus.

The religious spirit will rally allies in offense and anger. The Pharisees were outraged by Jesus's preaching and ministry, so they began to strategize in secret. Secrecy is one of the devil's great strategies. The enemy slithers around under the cover of darkness. His minions work best in hiding. The prophetic spirit boldly shines the light on hidden devils. That is why demons hate prophets, prophetic people, and prophetic ministry.

The god of this world has blinded the minds of those
who do not believe, lest the light of the glorious gospel of
Christ, who is the image of God, should shine on them.
For we do not preach ourselves, but Christ Jesus the Lord,
and ourselves your servants for Jesus' sake.
—2 CORINTHIANS 4:4–5

The gospel brings the light of God on the scene! Light
exposes the power of hell. The religious spirit operates with
secret councils, secret committees, and backroom deal makers.
They met in secret to attack Jesus. This is the game plan of the
religious spirit.

They were offended by truth yet honored dead traditions.
The religious spirit does not honor the Word of God. It twists
the Word of God to strip away the power of God. Religion establishes traditions without power. People go through the motions
without any results or breakthrough. Where the anointing is,
there is breakthrough and freedom!

For laying aside the commandment of God, you hold the
tradition of men—the washing of pitchers and cups, and
many other such things you do.
—MARK 7:8

**They held secret meetings joined together by a common
offense.**
When you remove the oil of Holy Spirit, there is a dry
atmosphere. Dry people are easily offended. I have never seen
a religious person, religious church, or religious ministry where
there is not an abundance of offense. God unites people by spiritual purpose, assignment, and legacy, but demons rally people
around anger, bitterness, and offense.

They used flattery to His face, yet their ultimate goal was to take Him out.

Devils will use flattery to speak to the egos of men and drive in a nail of bondage. They spoke to Jesus with the intent of flattering Him while secretly plotting against Him. Religious devils operate with a smooth tongue and a wicked plan.

The actions of the Pharisees displayed many attributes of the religious spirit. Let's explore some of the religious spirit attributes and how they manifest in the lives of believers.

NEGATIVE WORDS

The religious spirit comes with negative words. It loves to debate, argue, and pick apart every revelation and legitimate kingdom concept. It will twist Scripture in order to back its point. It will rip apart any person or ministry with a powerful anointing. It will defy all those with a prophetic spirit because it hates the flow. It wants to build religious camps of slavery and bondage. It will engage in endless disputes without ever moving in the power of God or anointing. Religious demons tell you why you cannot pray for healing, yet they have never prayed for a sick person in spite of the clear call of all believers to do so. Religious spirits will tell you why you cannot prophesy or how you did it incorrectly, yet they never have a prophetic word. Religious spirits will invalidate current cutting-edge ministries and wrap their offense in biblical language to hide their true intent.

The religious spirit condemns. Jesus came to set each of us gloriously free from condemnation and the works of the law. As we awaken to all that He is and all that He has called us to be, we step into a bold, uncommon realm of liberty. The religious spirit continually harasses and condemns people, placing value on judgment above mercy and blinding the eyes of its victims to the real power of the gospel.

> There is therefore now no condemnation for those who are in Christ Jesus, who walk not according to the flesh, but according to the Spirit.
>
> —ROMANS 8:1

The religious spirit also loves to complain and criticize. Wherever there is a religious spirit in operation, there will be critical attitudes in operation with much murmuring, complaining, and wrong speaking. Complaining is the language of hell. It empowers curses, bondage, fear, and contamination. Our mouths were created to be powerful weapons in the hands of the Lord. The religious spirit has no joy or victory; therefore it complains on a continual basis. Religious churches are always murmuring. They are never satisfied and manage to find something to be discouraged about. They create a toxic environment that kills dreams.

> Do not grumble against one another, brothers, lest you be condemned. Look, the Judge is standing at the door.
>
> —JAMES 5:9

PERVERSION AND COMPROMISE

The religious spirit is a spirit of perversion! One definition of the word *pervert* is "to twist the meaning or sense of."[1] Religious devils love to twist scriptures, bend truth, and alter the true meaning behind many kingdom concepts. The religious demon is a twisted devil. It binds people and turns the truth in order to deceive them. It leads to compromise by focusing on works without power. It creates a heart that is trapped in lifeless activity, easily opening the door to compromise. It abandons the plans of God in pursuit of building its own kingdom. Religion compromises the plans of heaven, the pathway of destiny, and the dream of God. It becomes so stuck in dead traditions that the life of the spirit is stomped out!

> Beware lest anyone captivate you through philosophy and vain deceit, in the tradition of men and the elementary principles of the world, and not after Christ.
> —COLOSSIANS 2:8

Where there is a religious demon, there is often an abundance of sexual perversion. People are so yoked with heavy bondage in every area of their lives that they begin to manifest deviant behaviors. The religious spirit robs people of the oil of spiritual intimacy and passion. It dominates their lives with ritual and no relationship. It overwhelms their souls with hardship and oppression. In the absence of relationship and an abundance of rules, it's easy to give way to impure desires and appetites.

There are some groups that will not allow you to preach without a uniform, yet it is no secret that some of their leaders engage in improper sexual relationships. In fact, sexual sin runs rampant in many of these groups because they are bound by the oppressive powers of the religious spirit. It is not what they wear, their tradition, or their practices that increase the level of carnality; it is the yoke of the religious spirit. Having a particular dress code is not a sin, but when a person or group places a demand on others to conform to their preferences and preaches hell on them if they don't, then you have the working of a demon of bondage. When the oil of Holy Spirit is removed, something moves in to fill the vacuum.

POLITICS AND CONTROL

The religious spirit is a political spirit. I am not talking about governing or world affairs but about political methodologies in kingdom ministry. The religious spirit values soulish ideas and control above strong Spirit leading. It plays politics in the church instead of hearing and releasing the fresh word of the Lord. When a place or a people becomes gripped by the religious spirit, it will become overly political, consumed and driven by the opinions of men. This type of atmosphere discourages daring spiritual leadership and radical obedience. It shuns strong prophetic preaching and bold ministry. It will stifle the flow and ministry of Holy Spirit to placate people and keep them in a false state of peace. The religious spirit is a master at control, binding and hindering regions.

The religious spirit places far too great an emphasis on keeping everyone happy. The reality is that when you boldly preach the gospel, prophesy, and cast out demons, there will be waves in the ministry. An apostolic or prophetic ministry will have warfare. It is impossible to advance in the spirit personally or corporately and not have some type of resistance. The religious spirit will try to contain and confine. Spirit life is about freedom and identity. The religious spirit places unholy limitations on people's lives, trying to mask their identity in Christ. This demon boxes in people, ministries, and groups. It places a lid on spiritual life. Religious spirits hate freedom! Their goal is to capture and contain people. The anointing brings freedom. The power of God breaks prison doors open!

> Now the Lord is the Spirit. And where the Spirit of the Lord is, there is liberty.
> —2 CORINTHIANS 3:17

No Joy

Religious people are angry people. They are offended by happiness, joy, and the preaching of the goodness of God.

> Clap your hands, all you people! Shout to God with a
> joyful voice.
> —Psalm 47:1

The Scripture tells us to worship God with exuberance and energy. Have you ever noticed how religious people value quiet and are offended by noise? Real praise is filled with emotion! There are emotions of thankfulness, gratitude, and excitement. As praise goes up, God's glory comes down, and people are shifted into the realm of the spirit. We were not created to offer God somber, unemotional praise and adoration. It is a shame that many people are OK with screaming, holding up signs, and dressing in uniform at a sporting event but totally irritated by bold and aggressive praise at a worship gathering. Oh, how shocked they will be when they get to heaven.

> Cry out and shout for joy, O inhabitant of Zion. For
> great is the Holy One of Israel in your midst.
> —Isaiah 12:6

> And those the Lord has rescued will return. They will
> enter Zion with singing; everlasting joy will crown their
> heads. Gladness and joy will overtake them, and sorrow
> and sighing will flee away.
> —Isaiah 35:10, niv

The Bible says that joy will crown our heads. We are to walk in the joy of the Lord. In fact, Nehemiah tells us that the joy of the Lord is our strength (Neh. 8:10). We can get through the battle with joy. Joy is a fruit of the Spirit, according to Galatians 5:22. As we spend time with Holy Spirit and live in the realm of the spirit, an overwhelming joy will come forth.

Joy is not connected to the ups and downs of life. There is a joy in the realm of the spirit that can be continual. The religious spirit stifles the joy of the Lord. It creates an atmosphere void of joy. It despises joy. Where there is joy, there is laughter. There is celebration. There is happiness and rejoicing—acting out the presence of joy. Religious demons create oppression, fear, and anger. In the camp of religion there is no room for joy or celebration.

Ungenerous

One time the Lord told me that if I wanted to locate the depth of the religious spirit in a region, just preach on the goodness of God and generosity. Angry people are not generous. Religious people get upset with stories of God's goodness and His provision. Religious demons hate preaching on provision because it is part of the revelation of God as our Father. A father provides, protects, and guides. Religious demons paint a false picture of identity.

> For the LORD your God has blessed you in all the works of your hands. He knows your wanderings through this great wilderness. These forty years the LORD your God has been with you. You have lacked nothing.
> —DEUTERONOMY 2:7

Over and over in Scripture God establishes Himself as our provider. One of the names of God, *Jehovah Jireh*, means "the Lord will provide." When we understand the role of our heavenly Father as provider, our faith is inspired, and we can dream big, believe big, sow big, and harvest big! Financial exploits are empowered by moving out of limitation and into the realm of generosity.

> But my God shall supply your every need according to
> His riches in glory by Christ Jesus.
> —PHILIPPIANS 4:19

We are called to live generously and give generously. This type of kingdom mentality breaks the back of poverty and fear in our lives. We no longer trust in ourselves or in this world's economy but rather in the abundant provision of heaven. We begin to move from fear and withholding the seed into faith and planting the seed with an expectation of supernatural harvest!

> There is one who scatters, yet increases; and there is one who withholds more than is right, but it leads to poverty. The generous soul will be made rich, and he who waters will be watered also himself. The people will curse him who withholds grain, but blessing will be upon the head of him who sells it.
> —PROVERBS 11:24–26

What leads a man or woman to transformative change?

> Do you despise the riches of His goodness, tolerance, and patience, not knowing that the goodness of God leads you to repentance?
> —ROMANS 2:4

It is the preaching of the goodness of God that positions a heart at the gateway of change. It is the revelation of the goodness of God that unfolds transformation. Understanding the abundance of God's goodness is a major key to moving into kingdom plans.

Think about it—how can you enter into exploits believing that God is mad at you and views you as a worm? The answer is simple: you cannot! A mentality of religion, fear, and false identity disempowers faith and massively fuels a fear mentality. You live your life as a series of works to earn a redemption that has already been paid for by Jesus in all of His glory.

Religion shackles you to the whipping post of failure. It provides an erroneous narrative of the greatest love story ever written. It convinces people who were eternally pursued, bought back, freed, and forgiven that God is angry and the plan unfulfilled. Many people are totally paralyzed by this toxic mind-set.

When we begin to hear, know, and understand the true nature of our Father, we become gloriously free. What do free men do? They dream immense dreams. They daringly step out to go for the seemingly impossible. This is why the religious spirit hates the message of the goodness of God—it leads people to freedom. When you discover what has already been done and who you are called to be, you will be well situated for an exhaustive metamorphosis.

> …making the word of God of no effect through your tradition, which you have delivered. And you do many similar things.
>
> —Mark 7:13

OPERATIONS OF THE RELIGIOUS SPIRIT

The religious spirit can operate on many different levels. There are two common operations. One is the level of personal attack, in which this demon goes after the hearts and minds of people who are on the verge of personal breakthrough. The other level is corporate attack, when the religious spirit targets those who hold power to transform the corporate body of Christ, the ekklesia.

Personal attack

Hunger is always that catalyst of change in the life of an individual. A person gets so hungry for the more of God that he or she becomes desperate. This is the gateway to progress. Our individual spiritual lives should look like a journey of personal advancement. We should never be content to just camp out where God met us last month or last week. Our prayer lives should be in motion. Our devotional lives should be in motion. Our prophetic lives (seeing, hearing, knowing) should be in motion. Our revelation should be increasing and evolving as the face of Jesus becomes clearer to us.

The Bible teaches in Matthew 5:6 that the hungry shall be filled. What about the satisfied? There is no account of provision for those who are complacent. Hunger and thirst are the picture of pursuit. Hungry people will travel. Hungry people will get up early in the morning. Hungry people will invest their lives in pursuit of heaven. I was recently reading the story of one of the great healing ministers of the previous generation. This man would preach with mind-blowing miracles erupting like a volcano. I wanted to know more. What was his secret? What was it that caused him to touch God in a way that touched a generation? What did he know about God that I did not yet know? What was the key that unlocked the door to another realm? So I started reading about his life. I quickly discovered the secret. He decided to pursue God until he found Him in all His miracle-working glory. He locked himself away for days and hours, praying until the Miracle Worker showed up. He got hungry and began to pursue God![2]

Make no mistake about it, that kind of pursuit infuriates the religious spirit. It will hurl condemning thoughts against a person who begins to chase God. It will release vile accusation and mind-tampering heaviness. It confines people on a personal basis to block their access to their spiritual inheritance. This is one level of operation. This is boots-on-the-ground combat.

Corporate attack

There is another level of warfare that the religious spirit engages in. It attacks people, leaders, revelation, offices, and wineskins that hold power to transform the corporate body of Christ. This is a higher level of strategic operation of the religious spirit. There are reforms that heaven releases on earth to suddenly shift the function, insight, and strength of the ekklesia. There are religious spirit high-level operations that create mind-sets, cultures, and concepts to keep the corporate body of Christ from moving forward.

Ultimately you cannot change the flow of the ekklesia until you change the function. Many times people cry, beg, and scream for an Upper Room outpouring. They desperately want Holy Spirit to pour forth fresh rivers and new wine, but they do not want to change the systems or structure of how they do things. Revival typically leads to a reform—a new order and new methods. Jesus taught about this very thing. He said that there could not be new wine without a new wineskin.

> And no one pours new wine into old wineskins, or else the new wine bursts the wineskins, and the wine is spilled, and the wineskins will be marred. But new wine must be poured into new wineskins.
> —MARK 2:22

New wine cannot be contained in an old wineskin. The old wineskin represents a fixed way of doing things. The reality is that God is continually opening our eyes to discover where He is moving and how we must move with Him. He shifts the wineskin before sending forth the burst of new wine. If He just sent the new wine, it would actually bring destruction to what has been built. There must be revelation of how to function. God raises up forerunners to tune in to His instruction and help His people embrace revelation to empower them to receive new wine.

We can see this pattern in Scripture when John the Baptist came on the scene preaching the message of the kingdom. He was preparing the people for a seismic shift, as Jesus would soon come announcing that the kingdom of heaven was at hand. The kingdom was there, standing right in front of them. The wineskin was shifting, but many would not shift. Then in the Upper Room the outpouring came and birthed the age of the ekklesia. There was a new wineskin. It would take apostolic fathers and mothers to articulate and teach the systems and structures that would appropriately steward the new wine.

This pattern continues today. Reform is birthed as God touches men and women to see in the Spirit, revealing His methods. There is reform happening with the purpose of abandoning the pathway of religion and embracing the plans of awakening. The unfolding of a new wineskin empowers God's people to receive a sustained release of new wine.

The religious demonic structures work overtime against the ekklesia to attack and persecute agents of change. They cite traditions and practices of man to overwhelm scriptural truth and prophetic leading. They fight like a religious mafia, debating, belittling, and tearing down to maintain business as usual. Many who are giving voice to it are deceived, just as Paul was before his encounter with Jesus on the road to Damascus. They believe that they are actually protecting the kingdom of God when, in fact, they are manifesting a religious spirit.

The late C. Peter Wagner masterfully articulates these truths in his book *Freedom From the Religious Spirit*:

> Daniel 2:21 tells us, "[God] changes the times and the seasons." Part of the character of God, then, is to continually produce new wine and to provide new wineskins for it. But Satan, of course, does not like that a bit, and later in the same book of Daniel, Satan reveals his purposes through the "fourth beast" who, according to the text, "shall persecute the saints of the Most High, and shall intend to change times and the law" (Dan. 7:25). What God designs for His glory and the advance of His kingdom, Satan constantly attacks in order to turn it back around.
>
> What device does Satan use to attempt to roll back God's new times and seasons? Look at that phrase "persecute the saints." The Aramaic word for "persecute" is *belah*, which means to "wear out" the mind. In other words, the corporate spirit of religion, as Satan's agent in this case, does not play so much on the heart or on the emotions or on personal holiness or on the fruit of the Spirit, but rather on the *mind*.[3]

TEACHING BRINGS LIBERTY

The work of the religious spirit on this level must be counteracted by teaching and training. Many moves of God are aborted too quickly by the attacks of a religious spirit. In the void of proper teaching, people succumb to the mental attacks of this demonic power.

My brothers, not many of you should become teachers, knowing that we shall receive the greater judgment. We all err in many ways. But if any man does not err in word, he is a perfect man and able also to control the whole body. See how we put bits in the mouths of horses that they may obey us, and we control their whole bodies. And observe ships. Though they are so great and are driven by fierce winds, yet they are directed with a very small rudder wherever the captain pleases. Even so, the tongue is a little part of the body and boasts great things. See how great a forest a little fire kindles. The tongue is a fire, a world of evil. The tongue is among the parts of the body, defiling the whole body, and setting the course of nature on fire, and it is set on fire by hell.

—JAMES 3:1–6

Those in the office of the teacher act as the rudder of a ship, turning the entire body. We will live and manifest what we believe. The way we change what we believe is through study—learning and renewing our minds. The teacher plays a key role in renewing the corporate mind of the body of Christ. High-level operations of the religious spirit will attack and attempt to discredit any teaching that holds the power to set people free. This demon knows that if people begin to think and believe differently, then they will move into transformation.

Teaching is essential to the formation, maintenance, and healthy establishment of new wineskins and new wine. Apostles receive heavenly communication and instruction to implement and build new-wineskin ministries for revelation in the body of Christ. Prophets release the revelation and decree of critical components of the new wineskins, but teachers fortify the wineskins with teaching, training, and building the walls, brick by brick, nugget by nugget.

In today's media-driven society, one of the religious spirit's favorite outlets is social media and online platforms. It will release lies against emerging voices and powerful kingdom leaders. It will attack their character, criticize their words, and attempt to tear down the revelation. It sees the threat and acts swiftly to stop it. Religious spirits attack any messenger who challenges their systems of bondage. People with religious demons will attack when they feel threatened by the revelation or ministry of another. Insecurity is always a breeding ground of demonic influence.

While most of these subjects relate to the attacks of the religious spirits on Christians individually and corporately, there is yet another dimension of the religious spirit. It binds the minds of the unsaved and keeps their hearts trapped in deception by partnering with a power called "doctrines of devils," actual demonic spirits that carry the message of false teaching to humanity to trap them outside of salvation. All people who dedicate their lives to the rules and regulations of any spiritual practice not built upon the cornerstone of Jesus and His salvation are being influenced by the religious spirit. The religious spirit works outside of the Christian church to build strong fortresses of false religion, creating men and women who are deceived and bound for hell but think they are on the road to heaven. It infiltrates politics and media and creates statements like, "All roads lead to heaven." These words are evil pronouncements of deception fostered by the powers of hell to convince mankind that they can be saved without the Savior and redeemed without the Redeemer.

False religions are empowered and established by demonic rulers. They create belief systems to keep people outside of heaven. They penetrate the thinking and believing of people to bind them to false ideas. Only the power of almighty God can break this type of religious deception. That is why it took a bright light and a Damascus road experience to reach Paul. He had to be convinced by the supernatural power of a living God. A living God speaks and moves!

POINTS TO CONSIDER

» Do I get jealous of others whom God is promoting?

» Am I spiritually dry? Does there seem to be an invisible lid on my spiritual life?

» Am I overly critical and too quickly distracted by meaningless debates?

» Am I stuck in dead traditions that do not lead me to the life of Jesus?

» Do I allow fear of man to hinder me and hold me back from moving in my calling?

» Am I easily offended?

» Do I really have the joy of the Lord in my life, or do I just do what is required of me to please others?

WHERE TO BEGIN

» Do a heart check every day.

» Learn to do everything for God alone, not to be noticed or praised by man.

» Ask God to reveal areas of bondage in your life and to show you how to escape.

» Encounter Holy Spirit on a continual basis to keep your oil flowing and your purpose pure.

» Be purposeful about recognizing patterns of religious activity with no spirit life.

» Release the oil of Holy Spirit in prayer and worship.

» Meditate on the goodness, generosity, and grace of God. Allowing His new nature to permeate your thinking will eradicate the power of the religious spirit in your life.

PRAYER

Father, keep me pure in all my motives. Show me if I ever begin to allow religion or bondage to enter my life. I want to serve You and You alone. I want only to please You, to do all I do for You. I am not a man pleaser but a God pleaser! You are the Author and Finisher of my faith. I break free from religious tradition and bondage in Jesus's name. I rip every demonic lid off my spiritual life, and I release Your abundant grace over me. I know that You are good, and I rest in Your goodness. I receive Your goodness. I confess Your goodness. I say that I am filled to overflowing with Your joy. Thank You, Lord, that I walk close to You all the days of my life, I hear Your voice, and You alone do I follow.

Chapter 9

FIRST-LOVE LIFESTYLE: FREEDOM FROM THE RELIGIOUS SPIRIT

I T IS IMPORTANT when examining properly the many-faceted dimensions of the religious spirit to begin with the understanding that there is a company of demons that make up this family of religious spirits. There are the religious demons that sow seeds of the world's false religions, as we established in the previous chapter. These devils work to abort the magnificent revelation of the man named Jesus Christ. In some regions of the world these demonic powers are so strong that the only way Jesus can break through is by visiting people in person through a vision, a dream, or even an encounter. The stronghold of false religion chokes out the preaching of the gospel, even threatening believers with acts of violence. This is one class of demon operating at a high level to restrict and rule a territory.

DON'T BE DECEIVED

Then there are the types of demonic beings that are most often associated with the term *religious spirits*. These spirits sow seeds of bondage into the lives of Christian believers. There are levels of assignment in that class of demon as well. There are the foot soldiers, or little demons, that influence the minds, thoughts, emotions, and belief systems of people. I remember a number of years ago dealing with one such devil. I was sharing with someone about the powerful ministry of Holy Spirit and speaking in other tongues. Without hesitation the person with whom I was sharing said that speaking in tongues was of the devil.

I asked why this person thought like that, and he rattled off what his church had taught and gave me a few opinions. I let him finish, and then I got out my Bible. I began to expound on the outpouring in the book of Acts. Then I went to commonly misunderstood scriptures in 1 Corinthians 14 and explained the diversities of tongues and the laws that govern each operation. I shared my personal testimony about all the miracles and breakthroughs I have had from praying in the Spirit. When I finished, the person was unwavering. "What about the Bible?" I asked. He had no answer. It was then I realized that his mind was twisted in knots and blocked to the truth by a religious spirit. This was the work of a demon that blocked the transforming knowledge of the Word of God.

Every one of us has had personal attacks from the religious spirit in our lives. We have been spoon-fed lies to keep us from kingdom living and victorious believing. I remember a time when I was in a revival meeting and Holy Ghost laughter broke out. The joy of the Lord hit the building as God began to minister to His people. I had never been in a meeting like that. It scared me, and I thought it must be of the devil. As I was trying to figure it out, the Lord rebuked me and told me it was Him moving! I quickly repented and jumped in the flow. That night my life was forever changed. As a matter of fact, nearly every breakthrough I have had in my journey with God has required me to face religious thinking and believing in order to go to the next level. I have had to determine that my heart is after God and I will be in the midst of His times, seasons, and activities in the earth. If I must change my mind-set, then I will! I will not get stuck.

There is an even greater measure of the religious spirit that acts to enslave groups of people in false belief systems and lifeless works. This type of spirit is a high-level demon most likely on the level of a principality, much like the queen of heaven (Jer. 7:18). This is a far greater plot than afflicting an individual with lust, rage, or despair. This is a territorial demon that infiltrates churches, ministries, groups, organizations, cities, and regions to establish firm strongholds of religious bondage. This demon has a collective assignment to ensnare and entangle a large group of people, thereby preventing the light of the gospel from spreading.

This ruling demon does not manifest boldly but hides beneath religious language and subtle attitudes. It seeks to establish a lid on a territory and people. It places a lid on the realm of power. Jesus preached the kingdom with power! The disciples preached the kingdom with power! The early church preached the kingdom with power! This high-ranking demon does all it can to dismantle kingdom thinking and structures as well as the power that they generate.

This demon deceives people into thinking they are doing God's will. It creates guardians that will fight with great intensity to maintain the religious status quo. One of the answers for this type of ruler is a true apostle who comes into a territory with a breaker anointing. (See Micah 2.) Apostles then break open the tough ground, preach with power, build a strong kingdom-based ministry, and establish spiritual sons and daughters. This demon, of course, will fight that type of ministry tooth and nail. Many regions with this type of religious spirit in operation have no strong apostolic or prophetic ministry. The religious churches and groups have run them all out of town.

WHERE THE SPIRIT OF THE LORD IS, THERE IS LIBERTY

There is no bigger aim of the religious spirit than to create enduring bondage. The aim of this demonic spirit is to undo the radical freedom that was obtained through Jesus's sacrifice at the cross.

> Now the Lord is the Spirit. And where the Spirit of the Lord is, there is liberty.
>
> —2 CORINTHIANS 3:17

The presence of the Lord breaks chains, tears down walls, and removes shackles. Religion hates spiritual freedom. It works overtime to reinforce evil and restrictive barriers.

The religious spirit creates a lack of freedom in the following:

- **Receiving God's love**—When you are bound, it is so difficult to know and believe the undying love of God.

- **Receiving God's goodness**—The nature of the Father toward His sons and daughters is that of goodness. Religious bondage empowers a theology that severely limits receptivity of the goodness of God. Believing, accepting, and receiving the goodness of God bring tremendous liberty.

> For freedom Christ freed us. Stand fast therefore and do not be entangled again with the yoke of bondage.
>
> —GALATIANS 5:1

- **Believing God's promises and who He says we are**—Bondage attempts to hold you away from the promises of God. We access breakthrough by accepting and acting on His promises. If you can find a promise from God, you can find a breakthrough.

  Religious bondage keeps people stuck in slavery when Jesus provided adoption into the family of God. A bound heart is a wounded heart! Breaking the grip of bondage releases tremendous healing and freedom of identity.

- **Prayer**—The religious spirit creates powerless patterns of prayer that resemble routine more than relationship. Prayer is intended to be an intimate method of communication. Freedom from religious bondage releases a heart to enter a deeper and more glorious communication with God. Breaking the bondage will release new dimensions of intimacy. One of the highest points of prayer is the release of glory. When we come into the presence of God and His glory shows up, He is there in person. When God steps in, anything is possible.

- **Relationship with others**—The religious spirit issues a constant stream of criticism and judgment, eradicating the grace of God. Bound people are continually judging others without any type of grace. True grace empowers love. When we walk in love, we are not easily offended. We are quick to forgive and full of mercy.

- **Walking in the power of God**—Religious bondage annihilates the flow of the power of God. It is impossible to believe God for miracles and breakthroughs when you are stuck in religious bondage. This demon is an anti-anointing demon. Reading and studying the miracles of Jesus build faith and create a paradigm of the power of God.

How can I personally overcome the prison of the religious spirit and the patterns of bondage? As with any deliverance, it begins with recognizing the patterns we have listed. These are the symptoms of a prison that the religious spirit has placed you in illegally. You must realize that this spirit infiltrates your thinking. In order to break free, you must be willing to think differently and look at the Word of God through a fresh lens.

Demon spirits travel through breaches. The dictionary defines *breach* as "a broken, ruptured, or torn condition or area."[1] It is essentially an opening. Deliverance requires expelling a spirit, breaking its grip by using the authority of the Word, the name, and the blood of Jesus to command it to go, and slamming every door shut to close the breach.

I remember a lady who struggled with condemnation and fear. She was invited to attend a meeting with a preacher who operated in a heavy religious spirit and released a very condemning message. One of my ministry team members advised her not to go and sit under that teaching. Why? Because it would only reinforce a mental and emotional opening that allowed demon spirits to travel back and forth. These openings must be closed by prayer and the Word of God. Every lie has to be addressed by the truth!

One of the great examples of this is the confrontation between Jesus and the devil in the wilderness. As Satan raged on with temptation after temptation, Jesus kept meeting his lies with the Word of God. Over and over again He stated, "It is written." He did not offer up His opinion or suggestion. He stood firmly upon the written Word of God. This is a victory key! Meet the lies with the Word. As you are breaking free from a religious spirit, you will have to refresh and renew your mind with the Word of God. You will have to speak God's promises of sonship and adoption over and over again.

Breaking free from the religious spirit will require purposeful pursuit of sonship. You must dive deep into the Scriptures to discover your identity as a son or daughter of God. You must build your faith by listening to teaching that reinforces your freedom. This will lead you to a place of unfettered worship that only sons and daughters enjoy. As you come into His presence from a place of freedom, you will soar above the bondage of the past.

Stay the Course

One way you can judge the strength of a revelation or a prophetic concept is the measure of resistance that it provokes. It is vital that you view the resistance as a confirmation and press on. The religious spirit blocks kingdom breakthrough by pressuring apostolic and prophetic ministry gifts to bow to dead traditions and humanistic opinions. The reality is that those very traditions act as tools to restrict and contain the move of God. We need daring apostolic leaders who refuse to bow and keep blazing the trail!

> When they had traveled through Amphipolis and Apollonia, they came to Thessalonica, where there was a synagogue of the Jews. According to his custom, Paul went in, and on three Sabbaths he lectured to them from

the Scriptures, explaining and proving that the Christ had to suffer and to rise from the dead, and saying, "This Jesus, whom I preach to you, is the Christ." Some of them were persuaded and joined with Paul and Silas, including a great crowd of devout Greeks and many leading women.

But the Jews who did not believe became jealous and, taking some evil men from the marketplace, gathered a crowd, stirred up the city, and attacked the house of Jason, trying to bring them out to the mob. But when they did not find them, they dragged Jason and some brothers to the city officials, crying out, "These men who have turned the world upside down have come here also."

—Acts 17:1–6

Paul and his team were directly challenging the ruling religious spirit, its false mind-set, its teaching, and the demonic grip it had on the region. What was the weapon of choice? Teaching! Paul expounded the truths of the Word of God in order to set the captives free. Breaking a ruling religious power will take teaching. There must be a release of heavenly foundations, a ripping apart of false foundations, and a building of new foundations. Apostles and prophets can work together to accomplish this goal in short order.

The region was stirred. This is the apostolic anointing in action. It breaks hard ground open, establishes the kingdom, and directly engages demonic rulers. Anytime there is an extreme reaction, it is evidence of spiritual warfare. The region rose and responded to the ministry of Paul. His ministry was not affecting just the ground but the airspace above where demons traffic.

The prophetic anointing carries such a grace to labor alongside apostolic ministry. Prophets carry an anointing to tear down the false! They prophesy against deception and reveal the testimony of Jesus.

> Then the LORD put forth His hand and touched my mouth. And the LORD said to me, "Now, I have put My words in your mouth. See, I have this day set you over the nations and over the kingdoms, to root out and to pull down, to destroy and to throw down, to build and to plant."
>
> —JEREMIAH 1:9–10

The Lord placed His word in Jeremiah's mouth to expose, confront, and tear down demonic structures, lies, and concepts. Prophets are spiritual warriors who do not back down from the threats of the enemy. They have seen the hidden demon crouching in the corner. They see the lie and refuse to keep silent. They become powerful weapons in the arsenal of the Lord. One deception that often grips prophets and prophetic people is that they become overly warfare oriented without revealing Jesus. It is critical that prophets understand the full weight of the call and their responsibility to love and serve the body as well as tear down. If there is no building, it becomes highly problematic.

> O foolish Galatians! Who has bewitched you that you should not obey the truth? Before your eyes Jesus Christ was clearly portrayed among you as crucified.
>
> —GALATIANS 3:1

Religious powers released a demonic enchantment over the Galatian church. Paul was speaking to them in a corrective fashion as their apostolic father. He could have used any language, but he chose to use the word *bewitched*. The purpose of this spell was to remove the believers from the liberty that had been established with the truth of the gospel and to replace truth with error, therefore shutting down the power and advancement of the kingdom.

How would this spell be broken? It needed to be addressed by the leaders and broken by the blood of the Lamb. Paul was exposing it in order to get them free. Exposure is warfare 101. You cannot conquer what you do not identify. Paul clearly marked the deception in order to bring the Galatians out of the snare of religious powers. This type of religious power moves to ensnare an entire group. It takes leadership within the group to renounce the authority of the enemy and break its power in the name of Jesus.

Many regions, organizations, and ministries need bold, strong leaders who will unashamedly rise up and break the powers of the enemy. God always appoints leaders to usher groups into the promise. There is an anointing that flows as pictured in Psalm 133. The precious oil of Holy Spirit flowed down upon the beard of Aaron the priest and onto the people. That type of anointing breaks yokes, restores vision, and empowers people. Every spiritual relationship should unlock a flow.

THE CALL OF FIRST LOVE

> But I have something against you, that you have abandoned the love you had at first. Remember therefore from where you have fallen. Repent, and do the works you did at first, or else I will come to you quickly and remove your candlestick from its place, unless you repent.
>
> —REVELATION 2:4–5

The church at Ephesus had forgotten its primary calling. It had abandoned the pathway of first love. There is a love that is to be above every other. There is a lover who paid the highest price for us. Our truest and highest calling is to love Jesus and be loved by Him—this is first love.

The entire mission of Christianity could be summed up simply like this: to be loved, to love God, and to love others. We are called to be living demonstrations of radical love, pursuit, and encounter. One of the deepest and most painful operations of the religious spirit is to trap us in a life of continual striving without truly experiencing the wonderful love and mercy of God.

But experiencing the wonderful love and mercy of God is our call! This is our passion—to live lives of first-love pursuit and encounter. Jesus did not come and willingly offer His life to make us good slaves. He came to seek and save that which was lost. The Father sent Him on a divine rescue mission to restore us back to the family of God.

> For the Son of Man has come to seek and to save that which was lost.
> —LUKE 19:10

> The mission of Jesus was to reposition us outside of the curse that resulted from the fall of Adam and to plant us in the family of God. He has delivered us from the power of darkness and has transferred us into the kingdom of His dear Son, in whom we have redemption through His blood, the forgiveness of sins.
> —COLOSSIANS 1:13–14

We have been radically delivered from the domain of darkness. We have been translated into the kingdom of God as sons and daughters. We are to live above the ruling powers of hell.

We are not to be bound by the schemes, plots, and lies of the enemy.

The religious spirit works to undo the reality of our new nature. When we were born again, we were essentially re-created. We have a new nature. We have a spirit that is made in the image and likeness of our Father. We are not limited. We are not under the realm of darkness or any of its regulations. We can live in the spirit realm. We can walk out the plans of God. We can live from the dimension of the glory of God.

> Do not lie one to another, since you have put off the old nature with its deeds, and have embraced the new nature, which is renewed in knowledge after the image of Him who created it.
> —COLOSSIANS 3:9–10

The religious spirit wants to set a trap for us as it did for the Galatian church. It wants to bind us in defeat and strap us down with bondage. We must make a concerted effort to tap into our new nature by walking in the Spirit. There is a pathway that leads directly out of bondage and straight into the wonders of the kingdom. This is the first-love lifestyle! Pursuit becomes the norm, and encounter is a regular occurrence.

To walk in the new nature, we begin with the understanding that we were saved not for works alone but for relationship. God's highest desire for our lives is relationship with Him. In order to understand the practical dynamics of what this looks like, we must first lay a foundation of what a relationship is. It begins with a bond and is strengthened by investment.

All relationships have some type of bond. Family relationships have a bond of blood. Romantic relationships have a bond of attraction and affection. Business relationships have a bond of benefit and shared goals. Our relationship with the Father is based on a bond of unwavering love and commitment.

> While we were yet weak, in due time Christ died for the ungodly. Rarely for a righteous man will one die. Yet perhaps for a good man some would even dare to die. But God demonstrates His own love toward us, in that while we were yet sinners, Christ died for us. How much more then, being now justified by His blood, shall we be saved from wrath through Him. For if while we were enemies, we were reconciled to God by the death of His Son, how much more, being reconciled, shall we be saved by His life. Furthermore, we also rejoice in God through our Lord Jesus Christ, through whom we have now received reconciliation.
>
> —ROMANS 5:6–11

God is so good that He pursued us even when we had no interest in serving Him. Time and again humanity failed God, but He pursued us anyway. This is the foundation of our relationship with the Lord. He loves us with a deep covenant love. He pursued us. He ransomed us. He forgave us, and He is presently working on our behalf. He is our good Father! This is the starting point of our relationship with Him—understanding His deep passion toward us.

He reconciled us. He brought us back into a position of sonship that Adam had forfeited. He paid it all for us. He provided His Son as a ransom for us. We begin our pursuit of God from a position of unfathomable love. We begin with the call of first love.

The Pursuit of God

Every relationship moves beyond a bond into pursuit. Any relationship that loses pursuit also loses encounter. These two are vital components of relationship. Pursuit demands that we take practical steps motivated by love. In our relationship with the Father we must develop a lifestyle of continual pursuit. What does this look like? Let me lay out some very simple and practical steps to living free from the grasp of a religious spirit and remaining planted in a first-love lifestyle.

- **Worship**—This is one of the distinguishing marks of a son or daughter of God. We are born to be worshippers. Worship is the act of releasing our intimate affection to the Lord. It is the expression of our adoration. Worship is the engine of first love. The Greek word for worship literally means "to blow kisses toward."[2] Worship is the language of heavenly love! We are releasing our affection and adoration toward Jesus, and as we sit in His presence, we are receiving His love back to us.

  Worship is the constant act of surrender. It is not just a few fleeting moments; it is a lifestyle of surrender. David is one of the Bible's great heroes. His source of power was his radical love for God. Time and again he was the underdog. He was the reject and the misfit, but he found the presence of God and was never the same. Worship, radical adoration, will crown the misfit and the underdog, taking them from pit to palace!

  We must develop a worship lifestyle. We lift our hands. We bow low before Him. We pour out our hearts. We worship with music. We sit in the quiet places, telling Him of our love. We surrender fully and deeply to Him. We feel His presence like waves rushing over us, encountering us, shifting us, refreshing us. This is worship! It is authentic, organic, and original. Make time for it, make space for it, and allow it to be a central focus of your life.

Bless the LORD, O my soul, and all that is within me, bless His holy name.

—PSALM 103:1

- **Praise.** What is the distinction between praise and worship? In many ways they flow seamlessly together, but there are some key differences. To praise is to lift up. Praise is lifting up the name of Jesus, the power of God, and the promises of God above every other thing. When we praise, we are exuberantly lifting up the Lord. Praise holds the power to crush the weapons of the enemy. Praise will break heaviness.

   Isaiah 61:3 tells us to put on "the garment of praise for the spirit of heaviness." Praise is an eruptive and exuberant expression of thanksgiving. When we praise God, we often begin from a place of remembering where and how He moved in our lives. This type of expression will create spiritual movement in your life. Every believer must be a praiser!

Praise the LORD! Praise God in His sanctuary; praise Him in the firmament of His power! Praise Him for His mighty acts; praise Him according to His excellent greatness! Praise Him with the sound of the trumpet; praise Him with the lyre and harp! Praise Him with the tambourine and dancing; praise Him with stringed instruments and flute! Praise Him with loud cymbals; praise Him with the clanging cymbals! Let everything that has breath praise the LORD. Praise the LORD!

—PSALM 150:1–6

- **Reading, studying, and meditating on the Word of God**—The Word of God is a manual straight from the heart of God. Romans teaches us that as we renew our minds with the truth of God's Word, we position ourselves to fulfill the will of God (12:2). Simply put, this means we must learn to think differently. That is a process, not a one-time thing. All believers must become students of the Word of God. They must read it regularly, study it, and dig into it. They must also meditate on it, ponder it, and pray it out.

  Isaiah 55:11 says, "So shall My word be that goes forth from My mouth; it shall not return to Me void, but it shall accomplish that which I please, and it shall prosper in the thing for which I sent it." The Word of God is our promise book. As we dive deep into the pages of the written Word, we are empowered to prosper and live from a place of victory. We can stand upon the promises of God and declare them over our lives. The Word will create strength, healing, and victory if we partner with it. We can receive it and decree it with great confidence. A journey into God's Word is an exploration of life-changing power. The Word of God is the voice of God in our lives. It is crafted to shape us and to plant us deep in the ways of our Father.

For the word of God is alive, and active, and sharper than any two-edged sword, piercing even to the division of soul and spirit, of joints and marrow, and able to judge the thoughts and intents of the heart.

—HEBREWS 4:12

- **Prayer**—Daily conversation, reflection, and communication with God is imperative to a vibrant first-love lifestyle. Volumes have been written about the various facets of prayer. There are so many pathways upon which we can travel into the heart of God. The primary thing is to make encountering and seeking God a priority. We need quiet times of prayer. We need times of governing prayer, of binding and loosing. We need times to lean in, be still, and listen. We need times of praying in the Spirit, building our faith, and unraveling the mysteries. Prayer was one of Jesus's most powerful weapons. When they were all looking for Him, He was alone, outside of the city pursuing the Father. This is our model. James 5:16 tells us, "The effective, fervent prayer of a righteous man accomplishes much." A life framed by prayer is one of powerful destiny fulfilled.

In the morning, rising up a great while before sunrise, He went out and departed to a solitary place. And there He prayed.

—MARK 1:35

SEEK HIM

A first-love lifestyle, free from the grip of religious deception, is one of pursuit. There are practical steps to build a life of ongoing relationship with God. When you pursue, you will find Him.

His power will show up. The men and women who do extreme exploits in a generation are those who have found His presence, His power, and His majesty. A first-love lifestyle creates a reservoir of power. Faith produces earth-shaking kingdom works.

> So faith by itself, if it has no works, is dead.
> —JAMES 2:17

This is the result of pursuit: the kingdom begins to manifest in your life, wonders are unlocked, and the supernatural comes bursting forth. This is what the religious spirit works overtime to stop. It does not want Christians operating in the power of the gospel with boldness, strength, and authority. It is impossible to hang out with Jesus and not manifest His power.

As you plunge headlong into the love of God, a deep well of His affection and nature will rise in your life. Love produces grace toward others. As God's love for you and toward you is unraveled, it becomes much easier to have grace and mercy for others when they fall short. The religious spirit has no grace with people. It uses rules and regulations to place shackles of bondage on people, but the love of God releases the grace and mercy of God.

> Be of the same mind toward one another. Do not be haughty, but associate with the lowly. Do not pretend to be wiser than you are.
> —ROMANS 12:16

Love produces personal freedom. As you discover how much God loves you, it sets you free from the lies, torment, accusation, and weapons of the enemy. The love of God acts as a powerful tool to enforce the revelation of freedom in Christ. The love of God empowers your identity as a son or daughter of God.

As you live a first-love lifestyle, you discover who you are! This breaks the chains of bondage and releases your heart to dream and believe big. The love of God creates a God-confidence in your life. You become convinced that God is ready, willing, and able to do all that He has promised. The impossible now seems to be within your grasp through the power of the name, the Word, and the blood of Jesus.

A life of first love plants you in a supernatural lifestyle. You begin to believe and expect the miracles of God. Your heart soars to believe for the miraculous. You step out of mundane, ordinary living and into the realm of the miraculous and extraordinary.

The goal of the religious spirit is to trap a believer into lifeless cycles in which he or she is unable to enjoy the privilege of intimacy with the Father. The work of Jesus on Calvary was total and absolute atonement. He paid the price for every human being who will receive Him. There is unfathomable freedom in the power of His blood.

Freedom is not a single moment but an ongoing journey. We move from faith to faith, from glory to glory. By the power of Holy Spirit, blinders are removed, and truth is made manifest. We have been positioned in Jesus in heavenly places and are called to rule and reign.

When we receive Jesus, we are made new. We receive a new nature that empowers us to live a life of the Spirit of God. Jesus's sacrifice gave us full access to the kingdom, to rule and reign with Him as sons and daughters of God. We can lay down the mentality of servanthood without sonship. We are empowered to rule and reign with Christ. We conquer and defeat the work of the religious spirit in our personal lives as we pursue the Lord, renew our minds, and take our places as sons and daughters, recognizing that we were born to live wildly and gleefully free!

POINTS TO CONSIDER

» Are you falling more in love with Jesus every day?

» Do you spend time with Him daily?

» Do you have a revelation of all that Jesus did for you?

» Do you honor Jesus by walking in the reality of all that He has secured for you?

WHERE TO BEGIN

» Spend time with Jesus, just talking with Him and listening. (Always have something to record what He says to you.)

» Meditate on the goodness of God, on the nature of God, and on all the promises for you.

» Read the Word of God for deeper revelation on the kingdom.

» Be vigilant about counteracting the lies of the religious spirit with the truth of the Word of God. Don't let the religious spirit put you and keep you in bondage.

PRAYER

Lord, give me a deeper revelation of Jesus and the price He paid for me. Show me how to walk in freedom in every area of my life. Give me understanding of reigning on this earth and of my identity as a son or daughter of God. I decree that I am free from sickness and disease, I have the mind of Christ, I am prosperous spirit, soul, and body, and I walk in all that the blood has purchased for me. In Jesus's name, amen.

Chapter 10

ENFORCING THE KINGDOM: LIVING FREE

THE MINISTRY OF Jesus brings deliverance. As He went forth in the earth, He broke the power of the devil.

> When Jesus entered Peter's house, He saw his wife's mother, lying sick with a fever. He touched her hand, and the fever left her. And she rose and served them. When the evening came, they brought to Him many who were possessed with demons. And He cast out the spirits with His word, and healed all who were sick.
>
> —MATTHEW 8:14–16

Everywhere Jesus went, people were delivered. The church has the same bold call to freedom in this hour. Yet as we look at the church today, most people either do not believe in casting out devils or have never been taught how to do it, and many think it is mere foolishness. Yet while they are asleep, the enemy advances.

We can no longer have a Pollyanna attitude and simply pretend the enemy is not real. But we also do not want to overemphasize his power. Though it is important for us to understand his schemes and know how to thwart them, we must remember that we are victorious and triumphant children of the Most High.

Someone once asked me, "Do you look for a devil behind every bush?" My answer: "No, but I know what to do when he shows up!" We can live free in our minds, free in our bodies, free in our spiritual lives, and free in every area! The total price has been paid.

No Longer Captive

If ever there has been a time for churches, ministries, and believers to be full of anointing, strength, and power, it is now! The world needs another great revival, but it is going to take a church on fire for that to happen. We must break the grip of these foul anti-anointing spirits and ride the mighty winds of God!

> For our fight is not against flesh and blood, but against principalities, against powers, against the rulers of the darkness of this world, and against spiritual forces of evil in the heavenly places.
> —Ephesians 6:12

Spiritual warfare is a part of our existence as believers. There are battles, attacks, and traps. We are not fighting with human beings but being resisted by unseen powers. Paul is teaching in these verses that there will be conflict. There will be opposition. Developing a winning strategy for war is critical. We cannot and must not leave our destinies to change. We cannot afford to shun the responsibility that we have as believers to engage the enemy and enforce the authority of the kingdom.

There are people who question the need for teaching on demon powers, bondages, and deception. If you were the devil and you really wanted to infiltrate culture, take over society, and bind up the church, what would be your master plan of deception? Convincing people that you are either not real or not doing anything would be a pretty good start. This is exactly what he does. He works overtime to strip revelation away from believers so that they will not pray in the Holy Spirit and move in the power of God. Their impotence allows him to operate subtly and effectively behind the scenes.

Effective warfare strategy begins with spiritual education. This is enforced time after time in the Bible. Paul admonished Timothy to be a good student.

> Study to show yourself approved by God, a workman who
> need not be ashamed, rightly dividing the word of truth.
> —2 Timothy 2:15

Learning the tactics of the enemy, the nature of demon powers, and the authority of the believer equips you for masterful and victorious warfare. Educating yourself prepares you for the task at hand.

You must also realize that demons prefer the cover of darkness. The devil functions best when he is unseen and hidden. He releases wicked schemes under the radar. Battle strategy number one is exposure! You can never overcome what you fail to identify. Discerning what type of demonic power you are facing helps identify its tactics, operations, and schemes. This also helps you know how to combat it.

Typically there are four points to break through a demonic attack. First, you discern the attack and identify the demon. Second, you enter into prayer to get wisdom and instruction. Third, you rise in authority to break the attack. You exercise the dominion that Jesus has given to you as a child of God. You boldly tell the devil no! You break his power and assignment over your life. You serve a spiritual eviction notice. This is what deliverance really is! It is evicting the enemy and sweeping the house clean.

Finally you renew your mind and develop your faith to stay free. It is one matter to get free, but you must realize that the devil is persistent. If a demon has been operating in and around you for years and then you evict it, it will look for a way to come back. Jesus taught us this principle. If people are not willing to do some follow-up work, then it is better not even to minister deliverance to them because they can end up worse off.

> When an unclean spirit goes out of a man, it passes through dry places seeking rest, but finds none. Then it says, "I will return to my house from which I came." And when it comes, it finds it empty, swept, and put in order. Then it goes and brings with itself seven other spirits more evil than itself, and they enter and dwell there. And the last state of that man is worse than the first. So shall it be also with this evil generation.
> —MATTHEW 12:43–45

We must recognize that deliverance is often a process and not a singular event. If people refuse to build their faith, study the Word, renew their minds, and fight the fight of faith, they can receive deliverance ministry and end up worse.

GO TO THE POWER SOURCE

I remember, a number of years ago as I was leading a church in a very religious territory, a severely bound man came to me for help. He told me that he had been molested as a child and had continual struggles. You could look at him and see the presence of an unclean spirit. It had attached itself to every part of his life. He was in desperate need of spiritual breakthrough and strong deliverance ministry.

I asked him where he went to church, and he told me. In that region there were few places that believed in and practiced deliverance. He was attending a nice church that had nice one-hour meetings with no power or authority. You may be happy to attend a nice church; you may love the music, the short services, and all the nice, predictable messages—until your family gets in trouble. Then you want a radical church that heals the sick, casts out demons, and believes in miracles.

I asked the man if he had shared this issue with his pastor. He said he had and that his pastor had laughed and said that they did not believe in demons at that church. This is a problem. If you have demonic oppression and you are attending a nice church that refuses to deal with demons, you can easily sink deeper into spiritual trouble. This man was desperate and in major trouble, but he was in a place that refused to help him. The reality of demons pushed them beyond their comfort zone.

You must understand that deliverance is neither pretty nor convenient, but it is absolutely necessary. The church you go to could be the difference between life and death for you.

It is easy to be extremely zealous, see a need, and just start casting out spirits, but in reality, if the person involved is not willing to do some follow-up work, you are doing that person a disservice. I have learned this the hard way. Demonic oppression creates strongholds in the thought life that act as gateways into a person. Those thoughts are connected to desires. The thoughts must be dealt with, the desires must be resisted, and the flesh must be put under. (Fasting is a great deliverance tool.)

The enemy will use thoughts, emotions, feelings, and desires to try and creep back in. Many people just want it all dealt with at an altar with no effort on their part. This is lazy faith! James taught us that faith takes some elbow grease. There must be some effort exerted. Not only do we have to break the foothold of the enemy, but we also must resist his attempts to come back.

> Therefore submit yourselves to God. Resist the devil, and he will flee from you.
> —JAMES 4:7

After receiving deliverance, the journey continues. It is imperative that you resist—stand against and firmly and repeatedly say no. It will take the prayers and agreement of others to keep the cord broken. Sometimes you must let go of some relationships and change your surroundings. You may have to stop watching certain programs and listening to certain music to slam the gateway shut and keep it that way.

The devil will lie to you and tell you that you are not free because you are having a tempting thought or desire. This is a heinous lie intended to overwhelm you and get you to give in to a spirit of defeat. You must recognize this lie and aggressively rise against it. You are not a captive to your mind, your body, or your appetites. You are in charge! You can use your authority to make these things line up with the Word of God.

> No temptation has taken you except what is common to man. God is faithful, and He will not permit you to be tempted above what you can endure, but will with the temptation also make a way to escape, that you may be able to bear it.
> —1 CORINTHIANS 10:13

The word *temptation* means "a strong urge or desire."[1] When a demon is removed, there can be root systems in the thought life. These thoughts attempt to give way to desires. These desires need to be bridled by the Word of God and your new nature. You must tap into the realm of the spirit and subdue the desire. The enemy provides temptation. Don't let the fact that you are being tempted cause you to question the freedom that belongs to you. The devil wants to use a fleeting thought or desire to convince you that you are bound. Do not buy his lies! Keep your confession strong and your mind rooted in the Word of God.

There is a powerful connection between what is in your heart and your mouth. When you believe something, you will think on it, and it will be planted deep inside of your thought life. You will then speak it out of your mouth. As you speak what you believe, you are releasing words of life or death in the realm of the spirit.

> Death and life are in the power of the tongue, and those
> who love it will eat its fruit.
> —PROVERBS 18:21

One vital key to living and staying free is to make speaking the Word of God part of your prayer life. Refuse to allow negative words of fear to dominate your mind and mouth. When the enemy screams at your mind that you are not free, boldly tell him that you are free and bind his lies up in Jesus's name! Dive deep into the Word of God, and find answers for your situation. Become a student of the freedom that you are seeking, and then pray, ponder, and meditate on those verses. Speak them out of your mouth. Call your mind free! Call your body free! Call your spiritual life free! Call your family free! Call your business, ministry, and financial life free! Prophesy the Word of God over your life by declaring what has already been written. Your mouth becomes a defense against the enemy.

Decreeing the victory and breaking the power of the enemy

are a crucial part of your personal freedom. Here are prayers and confessions for the various areas I have covered:

BREAKING JEZEBEL ATTACKS

Intimidation

Thank You, Lord, that You said in Proverbs 28:1 that the righteous are as bold as a lion! I break all intimidation from me in Jesus's name! I bind fear. I bind timidity in Jesus's name. I break the power of Jezebel's intimidation off my life in the name of Jesus. I command the lies of Jezebel to be broken off my mind. You foul Jezebel spirit, I command you to go, in Jesus's name. I will not listen to you. I will not surrender to you. I am free in the name of Jesus. Amen.

Rebellion

Lord, I thank You that I can and do fully surrender to You. You said in James 4:7 to submit myself to You and resist the devil. I come before You now, bowing my life before You. I offer myself as an offering to You. I give all of me to You. I repent for opening any doors of rebellion. I repent for partnering with rebellious thoughts or activities. I ask for Your mercy and forgiveness over my life in Jesus's name. I speak to every foul operation of rebellion, and I command it to go, in Jesus's name! I break the hold of Jezebel's rebellion over my life in the name of Jesus. I confess that I am free, that I honor authority and submit to all godly leaders, and that I live a life of godly surrender and submission in Jesus's name.

Word curses

Thank You, Lord, that I am blessed coming in and blessed going out, according to Deuteronomy 28. No curse can prosper against my life! I release the power of the blood of Jesus over me in Jesus's name. I break every word curse of Jezebel over my life. Every demonic decree over me is broken. Every false accusation is exposed and proved a lie. No lie will stand against me. No decree of witchcraft against me will prosper, in the mighty name of Jesus. I break the power of Jezebel over my life in Jesus's name! I say that I am free and the Word of the Lord is prevailing in my life in Jesus's name. Amen.

Confusion, manipulation, and lies

Thank You, Lord, that I walk in perfect peace, according to Isaiah 26:3. My mind is fixed upon You, Lord, and Your shalom is abundant in my life. I break every spirit and power of confusion sent from hell against me in the authority of Jesus's name. I break the power of lies and confusion from the Jezebel spirit. I break manipulative powers over my life in Jesus's name! I say that I am free from guilt, shame, and control. I refuse to manipulate others and strive to get my own way. I command all powers of manipulation to be broken over my life in Jesus's name. The Jezebel spirit has no authority over my life. I command every form of Jezebel witchcraft and attack to be broken in Jesus's name. Amen.

Strange fire

Thank You, Lord, that I am consumed by Your holy fire in Jesus's name, according to Hebrews 12:29. The fire of purity prevails in my life. The fire of revival is burning in me. The fire of awakening is rich in my life. The fire of deliverance and power is strong in me. I break every attack of strange fire and sorcery over my life. No strange fire can enter my life, in Jesus's name. I break the power of Jezebel's witchcraft over my life in the mighty name of Jesus and command it to go right now. I loose the freedom and purity of the Lord Jesus Christ in every area of my life. I say that I am blessed and free in the name of Jesus. Amen.

Seduction

Thank You, Lord, that I am pure in my thought life. Thank You, Lord, that I am sexually pure. I break all thoughts and temptations of lust in the name of Jesus. I break every spirit of perversion off my life and command them to go now in Jesus's name. I am not seduced or drawn away by the Jezebel spirit. I release the holiness and purity of the Lord over my life. Lord, You said in 1 Thessalonians 4 that I should be sanctified and avoid all immorality. I call for purity in my life. I consecrate my mind and body to You in the name of Jesus. Lust cannot operate in me. Immorality cannot prevail in my life in Jesus's name. I release the power and freedom of Jesus in my life right now. Amen.

Breaking Python Attacks

Physical attacks

Thank You, Lord, that I am healed and free. I break every attack of choking, congestion, and breathing problems in the name of Jesus! I say that I am healed and free. According to Job 33:4, "The Spirit of God has made me, and the breath of the Almighty has given me life." I thank You, Lord, that my breathing is normal! You foul python spirit, I command you in the name of Jesus to take your hands off my body. I command you to loose my lungs, throat, and breathing. Go now, in Jesus's name! I say I am healed and free by the blood of Jesus Christ. Thank You, Father, for Your power flowing over my body now in Jesus's name. Amen.

Confusion and heaviness

I come against confusion, in Jesus's name! I break the power of the python spirit over my thought life. I release supernatural peace in the name of Jesus. I boldly confess that I have the mind of Christ, according to Philippians 2:5. My thoughts are clear. My thoughts are filled with the knowledge of God. I also break heaviness and confess that I am filled with joy. Python spirit, I break your grip over my thoughts and emotions in the name of Jesus! I command you to go right now, in Jesus's name. I say that I am free. I say that I have the joy of the Lord. I say that I am blessed now in Jesus's name. Amen.

False utterances and false prophetic words

Father, I thank You for purity in every area of my life in Jesus's name! You said in Your Word that the spirit of prophecy is the testimony of Jesus (Rev. 19:10). I break every false prophetic word over my life in Jesus's name! I pull down every misleading and destructive utterance. I bind up every wrong decree, and I release the power of the blood of Jesus over my mind. I thank You, Lord, for cleansing my prophetic life so that I hear Your voice and align with Your will. I command every lie of python over my life to be broken now in Jesus's name! I command every false prophetic spirit to go now in Jesus's name. I thank You, Lord, that I am free in Jesus's name. Amen.

Flattery

I break every flattering lie that has been spoken over me. In James 4:10 You said, "Humble yourselves in the sight of the Lord, and He will lift you up." I come before You now, humbly asking for Your direction and guidance in every area of my life. I thank You, Lord, that my heart is fully surrendered to You in Jesus's name. I command every flattering decree of python to be broken over my life in Jesus's name. I break every deceptive word in Jesus's name. I command the power of the python spirit over me to be broken right now in the mighty name of Jesus. Amen.

Stalking

Thank You, Father, that according to Psalm 37:23, my steps are ordered of the Lord. You have provided the right steps for me to take in every area of my life. I am confident in Your leadership and guidance. I am protected and loved by You as I follow Your leading. I break the stalking spirit of python over my life in Jesus's name! I am not harassed, followed, or irritated by the python spirit. Python spirit, I command you to go now, in Jesus's name! I confess that I am free. My steps are blessed, and my pathway, secure in the name of Jesus. Amen.

Lies and deception

Thank You, Lord, that I am led by Your Spirit, according to Romans 8:14. The Holy Spirit lives in me. The Holy Spirit is my teacher. I am not deceived. Deception cannot prevail in my life. I break the power of deception and deceiving spirits in the name of Jesus! I break lies and false thoughts off my life. I command the power of every lie to be broken in the mighty name of Jesus. I confess that the anointing lives in my belly, according to 1 John 2:20. The Spirit of truth lives in me, and I am led into all truth. I am not deceived. I break free from the grip of python in the authority of Jesus's name. I command the spirit of python to go from every area of my life now in Jesus's name! Spirit of python, I cast you out right now! Leave in the authority of the Lord Jesus. I am free in Jesus's name. Amen.

BREAKING RELIGIOUS SPIRIT ATTACKS

Complaining

Lord, I choose to meditate on Your goodness in my life. I am so thankful for every blessing, every miracle, every breakthrough—even the little things. I confess that You are my Father. You are my healer. You are my provider. You are my everything. You said in Philippians 2:14 that I should do all things without murmuring or disputing. Thank You, Father, that my mouth is filled with praise and my heart is filled with thanks. I rebuke the religious spirit and command its power over my life to be broken in the name of Jesus. I cast out the religious spirit now and break it off me in the mighty name of Jesus. Amen.

Offense

Thank You, Lord, that I walk in love. You said in 1 Corinthians 13 that love is patient and kind. I confess that I am patient with others and I am kind. I do not keep track of wrongs. I do not hold grudges. I am free from offense. I break the power of offense off my life in the name of Jesus. I choose to walk in forgiveness toward others. I choose to release all pain and wounds. Father, I thank You for Your nature, Your love, and Your mercy operating in me toward others. I release all hurts, and I declare Your love is washing over me now in Jesus's name.

Critical attitude

Thank You, Lord, that You said in 1 Corinthians 13 that love never fails! I say that I walk in love and mercy with people. I say that I see Your love for their lives. I say that I see the potential in people. I see the victory in their lives. I am not critical, in the name of Jesus. I break every critical attitude and thought process over my life. I refuse to partner with the religious spirit and have a negative attitude. My eyes see as Christ would see. My mouth speaks as Christ would speak. I walk by faith and not by sight in the name of Jesus! I am free in Jesus's name. Amen.

Condemnation

Thank You, Lord, that I am free from condemnation as a child of God, according to Romans 8. I break every lie that would try to condemn me or accuse me in the name of Jesus. There is no condemnation in Christ Jesus! The Spirit of life has made me free. I am free in my mind! I am free in my spirit! I am free in my body! I walk in Your grace. I receive Your promises. I receive Your goodness and Your love in my life. I break the weight, the lies, and the hindrance of condemnation off my life in the name of Jesus. I command condemnation to go in Jesus's name! I break every religious lie and mentality off my life and boldly declare that I am blessed, loved, forgiven, accepted, and free in the name of Jesus. Amen.

Dryness

Thank You, Lord, for the rivers of living water in my belly, according to John 7:38. I call forth Holy Spirit rivers in my life. I break the dry climate that Jezebel and religion would attempt to establish in my spiritual life. I release the rivers of refreshing. I release the rivers of joy. I release the rivers of healing. I release the rivers of mercy. I release the rivers of restoration. You said that You would anoint me with fresh oil. I declare fresh Holy Spirit oil running over every area of my life in the name of Jesus! Thank You, Father, for the outpouring of Your spirit in my life. I break and bind the weight of the religious spirit and every religious attack, and I cast them out of my life in the name of Jesus! I command them to go now in Jesus's name. I call forth a spiritual climate shift in my life in the name of Jesus. Amen.

Bondage

Father, I thank You that Jesus paid the price for freedom in every area of my life. You said in John 8:36 that he whom the Son sets free is free indeed. I claim absolute freedom from all forms of religious bondage. I break heaviness and bondage off my thought life in Jesus's name. I break bondage off my spiritual life in Jesus's name. I release the power of God over me. I decree total freedom through the blood of Jesus. I am not bound; I am free. I command the religious spirit to go now, in the name of Jesus—I cast you out and break your power over my life. As I read the Word of God, I say that I read it as a son or daughter and not a slave. I say that my mind is being renewed and my thoughts are lining up with Your promises. I release freedom over every area of my life in Jesus's name. Amen.

As you break the power of these demonic spirits over your life, you are invoking the rights and privileges afforded you by the shed blood of Jesus Christ. Authority must be exercised. The enemy will always attempt to overstep and push the limits. Establishing yourself in the revelation of your identity and freedom powerfully positions you to live without the evil influence of the #ToxicTrio.

199

NOTES

INTRODUCTION

1. *Merriam-Webster,* s.v. "conspire," accessed October 30, 2017, https://www.merriam-webster.com/dictionary/conspire.

CHAPTER 1
THE REALITY OF THE UNSEEN REALM

1. *Merriam-Webster,* s.v. "dwell," accessed October 20, 2017, https://www.merriam-webster.com/dictionary/dwell.
2. John Eckhardt, *Prayers That Rout Demons* (Lake Mary, FL: Charisma House, 2008), 1.
3. Blue Letter Bible, s.v. *"energeō,"* accessed October 20, 2017, https://www.blueletterbible.org/lang/lexicon/lexicon.cfm?Strongs=G1754&t=KJV.
4. *HELPS Word-Studies,* "1754. *energeō,"* Bible Hub, accessed October 20, 2017, http://biblehub.com/str/greek/1754.htm.
5. James W. Goll, *The Seer Expanded Edition: The Prophetic Power of Visions, Dreams, and Open Heavens* (Shippensburg, PA: Destiny Image Publishers, 2012), chapter 2, https://books.google.com/books?id=CYc0IQx9q2kC&q.

CHAPTER 2
THE POWER OF THE ANOINTING

1. Benny Hinn, *Operating in the Anointing* (Bookmark Publishing, 2017), Lesson 1, https://bennyhinnbiblestudy.org/course/operating-in-the-anointing/.

CHAPTER 3
JEZEBEL, THE SPIRITUAL ASSASSIN

1. *Merriam-Webster,* s.v. "rebellion," accessed October 23, 2017, https://www.merriam-webster.com/dictionary/rebellion.

CHAPTER 4
JEZEBEL'S SEDUCTION, SCHEMES, AND STRATEGIES

1. Blue Letter Bible, s.v. *"tithēmi,"* accessed October 23, 2017, https://www.blueletterbible.org/lang/lexicon/lexicon.cfm?Strongs=G5087&t=KJV.
2. Blue Letter Bible, s.v. *"prōton,"* accessed October 23, 2017, https://www.blueletterbible.org/lang/lexicon/lexicon.cfm?Strongs=G4412&t=KJV.
3. Blue Letter Bible, s.v. *"archē,"* accessed October 23, 2017, https://www.blueletterbible.org/lang/lexicon/lexicon.cfm?Strongs=G746&t=KJV.
4. Blue Letter Bible, s.v. *"exousia,"* accessed October 23, 2017, https://www.blueletterbible.org/lang/lexicon/lexicon.cfm?Strongs=G1849&t=KJV.
5. *Merriam-Webster,* s.v. "seduce," accessed October 23, 2017, https://www.merriam-webster.com/dictionary/seduce.
6. Jennifer LeClaire, *Jezebel's Puppets* (Lake Mary, FL: Charisma House, 2016), 41.

CHAPTER 5
CASTING DOWN THE DEMON QUEEN JEZEBEL

1. "Jezebel Meaning," Abarim Publications, last updated September 1, 2017, http://www.abarim-publications.com/Meaning/Jezebel.html#.We5AsGhSwdU.
2. "Jezebel No. 1," *All the Women of the Bible*, Bible Gateway, accessed October 23, 2017, https://www.biblegateway.com/resources/all-women-bible/Jezebel-No-1.
3. John Paul Jackson, *Unmasking the Jezebel Spirit* (Flower Mound, TX: Streams Ministries International, 2002), chapter 2, https://books.google.com/books?id=3nFVDQAAQBAJ&q.
4. Blue Letter Bible, s.v. *"apostolos,"* accessed October 23, 2017, https://www.blueletterbible.org/lang/lexicon/lexicon.cfm?Strongs=G652&t=KJV.

CHAPTER 6
PYTHON, THE HEAT-SEEKING DECEIVER

1. Ruth Ward Heflin, *Revival Glory* (Morrisville, NC: lulu.com, 2013), 154, https://www.amazon.com/Revival-Glory-Ruth-Ward-Heflin/dp/1304256162.

2. Bible Hub, s.v. *"ruach,"* accessed October 24, 2017, http://biblehub .com/hebrew/7307.htm.

3. Blue Letter Bible, s.v. *"pythōn,"* accessed October 24, 2017, https:// www.blueletterbible.org/lang/lexicon/lexicon.cfm?Strongs =G4436&t=KJV.

4. "Apollo," *Encyclopedia Mythica,* last modified January 31, 2004, accessed January 3, 2018, http://www.pantheon.org/articles/a /apollo.html.

5. See, for example, Euripides, *Andromache,* line 1106, https://books .google.com/books?id=zws69QCKDAMC&pg.

6. Kevin Kleint, "Introducing the Oracle at Delphi," HonorOfKings .org, June 23, 2017, https://www.honorofkings.org/python-spirit -oracle-delphi/.

7. Jennifer LeClaire, *The Spiritual Warfare Battle Plan* (Lake Mary, FL: Charisma House, 2017), 40.

CHAPTER 8
THE DNA OF THE RELIGIOUS SPIRIT

1. *Merriam-Webster,* s.v. "pervert," accessed October 24, 2017, https:// www.merriam-webster.com/dictionary/pervert.

2. A. A. Allen, *The Price of God's Miracle Working Power* (Memphis, TN: Bottom of the Hill Publishing, 2012).

3. C. Peter Wagner, "The Corporate Spirit of Religion," in *Freedom From the Religious Spirit* (Bloomington, MN: Chosen Books, 2014), https://books.google.com/books?id=wLMlBQAAQBAJ&q.

CHAPTER 9
FIRST-LOVE LIFESTYLE: FREEDOM FROM THE RELIGIOUS SPIRIT

1. *Merriam-Webster,* s.v. "breach," accessed November 8, 2017, https://www.merriam-webster.com/dictionary/breach.

2. Blue Letter Bible, s.v. *"proskyneō,"* accessed November 29, 2017, https://www.blueletterbible.org/lang/lexicon/lexicon.cfm?Strongs =G4352&t=KJV.

CHAPTER 10
ENFORCING THE KINGDOM: LIVING FREE

1. *Merriam-Webster,* s.v. "temptation," accessed October 25, 2017, https://www.merriam-webster.com/dictionary/temptation.

Ryan LeStrange is an apostolic and prophetic revolutionary, laboring to see global awakening. He moves strongly in the power of God traveling the globe to ignite revival fires and build a growing apostolic-prophetic movement. His conferences and gatherings are alive with prophetic declaration, miracles and healings, fire, and powerful preaching.

Ryan is the founder and apostolic leader of a global network of ministries known as TRIBE Network. He is a cofounder of AwakeningTV.com, a media channel created to host revival-inspired services featuring ministers and messages both past and present. He is the senior leader of the iHub movement, planting and overseeing a network of governing churches, apostolic hubs, and revival hubs. Ryan is also a real estate investor, active in the business arena.

Ryan is a best-selling author. His books include *Supernatural Access, Overcoming Spiritual Attack, Releasing the Prophetic,* and *Revival Hubs Rising,* which was coauthored with Jennifer LeClaire.

Ryan and his wife, Joy, have one son, Joshua, and currently reside in Virginia.

INVITE RYAN @ ryanlestrange.com

 Instagram @ryanlestrange

 Twitter @RyanLeStrange

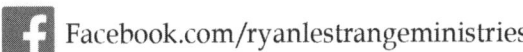 Facebook.com/ryanlestrangeministries

 Youtube.com/user/TheRyanLeStrange

 Ryan LeStrange
M I N I S T R I E S
P.O. BOX 16206 | BRISTOL, VA 24209